THE MOSCOW
KREMLIN

A Guidebook

D1445677

The Moscow Kremlin
State Historical and Cultural
Museum-Monument

УДК 719(470-25)(036)
ББК 85.101(2-2Москва)Я2
　　　М82

This Guidebook will familiarise you with milestones in the history of the Moscow Kremlin, inseparable as it is from the history of the Russian state, and introduce you to the architectural monuments and the unique exhibits displayed at the world-famous museum.

Numerous photographs and reproductions provided in this Guidebook show selected masterpieces from museum collections and offer an overview of modern-day and antique edifices and interiors of the Kremlin.

The book is supplemented with detailed maps and ground plans of the Kremlin premises and the Armoury and is appended with a glossary of terms.

ISBN 5-88678-060-2

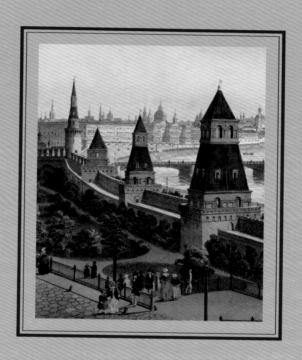

THE CITADEL
OVER THE MOSKVA RIVER

The Moscow Kremlin is the town-forming nucleus of Moscow, the starting point of the city's history, Russia's stronghold and spiritual hub.

History willed it that a humble Slav settlement in the backwoods of the Vladimir Principality should grow into a centre of north-east Rus and later become the capital of the biggest state in medieval Europe.

The Moscow Kremlin stands on the left bank of the Moskva River where it is joined by its tributary, the Neglinka. The area occupied by the Kremlin within the confines of the fortified wall is 27.5 hectares. The elevation of the **Borovitsky Hill** that Kremlin stands upon is 25 metres. Supposedly, the hill took its name from the ancient settlement of *Bor* or *Borovichi*.

In its outline, the Kremlin resembles an irregular triangle. It extends 676 metres from west to east and 639 metres from north-west to south-east. Because of its extremely advantageous geographical position at the crossroads of land routes and waterways converging at the foot of the hill, the settlement had from times immemorial been a hub of crafts and trade. The Slav tribe of *Vyatichi* inhabited this area in the olden times.

The early periods of Moscow's and the Kremlin's history were inseparable. It is believed that both came into being on the 4th of April 1147 when the son of the Kievan Prince Vladimir Monomachus, Yuri, nicknamed Dolgoruky (Long-Armed) for his ambition to spread his power to other principalities, invited his ally Prince Svyatoslav Olgovich to visit Moscow, on his way back from a military campaign.

However, as the well-known scholar, historian and archaeologist I.Ye.Zabelin noted, *"The Moscow community and specifically the Kremlin settlement had emerged long before the area was populated by Prince Ryurik's tribe"*. That theory was supported by the archaeological excavations at the Borovitsky Hill. Its underside had from olden times attracted the seekers of hidden treasures, caches of valuable items and the famous library of Ivan the Terrible.

Excavations begun by the Institute of Archaeology of the USSR Academy of Sciences and the Museum of the History of Moscow marked the starting point of truly scientific research, now taken over by The Moscow Kremlin State Historical and Cultural Museum-Monument. Every year brings in more

Prince Yuri Dolgoruky's encounter with Prince Svyatoslav Olgovich. Miniature from the Illustrated Chronicles of the 16th century.

reliable data increasing our knowledge of the early history of the city of Moscow and the Kremlin.

The Borovitsky Hill bears the imprints of various epochs. The most ancient archaeological discoveries include a stone battle axe dating back to the end of the 3rd — the middle of the 2nd millennia, typical of the Bronze Age artefacts frequently found in similar mounds. At the beginning of the 1st millennium, the area where the mod-

The "Archaeology of the Moscow Kremlin" exhibition in the basement of the Cathedral of the Annunciation.

ern-day Kremlin stands was the site of a fortified settlement typical of the early Iron Age.

Most of the excavated items, now on museum display in the Kremlin, are artefacts of the material culture of the Middle Ages. Archaeology, the "enigmatic female parent of History" provides first hand evidence of the city's development, the domestic detail of the first Kremlin settlers' everyday life, the techniques of major urban crafts, trade links, life style, dress and personal adornments of the Moscow residents.

The Kremlin's ***first wooden fortification*** is dated by the chroniclers at 1156. The remains of its walls are listed among the most valuable archaeological finds.

The Kremlin wooden structures would be frequently destroyed by devastating fires, enemy attacks and natural disasters. Moscow was razed in the first third of the 13th century when the Mongol-Tatar hordes invaded Rus ravaging the country with sword and fire. At that time, Moscow was an outlying suburb of the capital city of Vladimir

*The Moscow Kremlin in the time of Ivan Kalita.
A watercolour painting by A.M.Vasnetsov. 1920s.*

while the Kremlin with its prince's court, old churches, residential and administrative buildings was an outpost fortress at the outskirts of the Vladimir principality. The Moscow stronghold was the first to take the devastating attack of the nomadic armies. The Kremlin was burned to ashes. Remarkably, only one out of the six Mongol princes who led the invading armies into Europe was killed during the campaign and his blood was spilt in a battle near the Kremlin.

The underground caches buried about 800 years ago and unearthed by archaeologists provide material evidence of the ordeals undergone by the Kremlin. The 24 Kremlin caches contained old scriptures and weapons, jewelry and old coins. Today, all those items are part of the old Russian art repository and occupy an important place in the Kremlin museum showcases.

In the 14th century Moscow set foot in the arena of the world history. The city grew and became richer. In 1339, Prince Ivan Kalita had a new wall of oak wood fortifications constructed around the Kremlin, transforming it into a formidable medieval fortress. A contemporary chronicler wrote, "*...the city of Moscow is of great size and majestic appearance, abounding in rich and eminent people and surpassing in its fame every other city in the Russian land...*" It was at that time that the Kremlin (derived from the old Russian *kremnik* – fortress) was first mentioned in the Russian chronicles. Thus, the Voskresensky Chronicle dates the *city of Kremlin* at 1331.

The city of Moscow that took the lead in the unification of fragmented Russian principalities into a single centralised state grew and improved its looks. The city's wooden buildings would, however, often fall victim to devastating fires. The great fire of 1365 razed the Kremlin to the ground.

As the city needed stronger defences, the young Prince Dmitry Ivanovich, grandson of Ivan Kalita, ordered *stone fortifications* to be constructed around the Kremlin.

Those walls became the first-ever stone fortifications in Vladimir-Suzdal Rus. On two occasions (in 1368 and 1370) the formidable fortress was able to withstand sieges by the troops of the Lithuanian Prince Olgerd. Guarding the rear, the white-stone Kremlin citadel made it possible for the troops led by Prince Dmitry to openly challenge the Horde's domination and gain a glorious victory in the battle at Kulikovo Pole on the 8th of September 1380, putting an end to Russian humiliation. No evidence has been preserved as to what the Kremlin wall and towers looked like in the time of Dmitry Donskoy (the surname assumed by him in the wake of the Kulikovo battle). Conceivably, 5 out of 8 or 9 towers had gates, 3 of them facing the Red Square. White stone mined near the village of Myachkovo in the vicinity of Moscow served as the building material for the Kremlin fortifications.

Towering over Dmitry Donskoy's golden-domed palace was the Cathedral of the Saviour of Transfiguration in the Bor (Forest), built back in 1330 in the time of Ivan Kalita. Later, a monastery was founded there. The Spassky (Saviour's) Cathedral served as the burial place for grand princesses. The cathedral is also known as the seat of the Moscow chroniclers. Other cloisters were built in the area over time such as the Chudov Monastery, (1358) and the Voznesensky Convent (1386). The Cathedral of the Miracle of Archangel Mikhail was built of stone in 1365.

Although the Moscow's first stone buildings reflected the Vladimir-Suzdal architectural style, they did not duplicate it. The single-domed church design with Vladimir-style facades ornamented with *kokoshnik*-shaped ogee gables and carved friezes, would later become the mainstay of the Moscow architecture. The above-ground portions of those buildings did not survive. Their architectural appearance can only be conceived from the carved white stone fragments showcased at the Belfry of Ivan the Great.

The murals inside the first Moscow churches were painted by best Russian and Greek artists including the famous painter Theophanus the Greek. *Tall iconostases*, a specifically Russian form of church interior adornment, began to be constructed at the Kremlin churches during the late 14th – early 15th centuries. Andrei Rublev elevated the old Russian pictorial art with his great icons created during the late 14th – early 15th centuries.

The late 14th – early 15th centuries marked a crucial period in the development of the Russian national art and cultural tradition. During that time the local architectural schools merged together to form the single national school of architecture.

The Grand Prince Ivan III (1462-1505) who took the title of the "Tsar of all Russia", completed the unification of independent principalities into a single centralised state. The development of the single Russian state and the growth of its international credibility was bolstered by the official ideology that unconditionally recognised Rus-

The Moscow Kremlin in the time of Ivan III.
A watercolour painting by A.M.Vasnetsov. 1921.

sia as the successor of the world's largest kingdoms – the Roman and the Byzantine empires – and referred to Moscow as Third Rome.

The Moscow residence of the Grand Prince put on particular lustre and splendor under Ivan III. The year 1485 saw unprecedented new construction launched on the Kremlin premises.

The *red-brick Kremlin wall* built back in those times has survived to date. It was adapted to accommodate the already established area planning patterns and its shape was that of an irregular triangle extending through the perimeter of 2,235 metres.

Circular towers stand at the corners of the fortress with rectangular gate-towers in between. The wall height varies from 5 and 19 metres and its thickness from 3.5 and 6.5 metres. On top of the wall there is a firing gallery from 2 to 4.5 metres wide, protected on the outside with battlements (*merlons*) and provided with slit-like embrasures. In all, there are 1,045 merlons on the wall. The towers used to be topped with tent-shaped wooden roofs and lookout posts. Several towers were equipped with alarm bells and clock chimes. In he old days, the wall of the fortress was topped with a wooden gable roof.

The fortifications were constructed on a phase-by-phase basis. The construction began from the southern flank where the threat of an attack by nomadic armies was the greatest.

The first tower built there in 1485 by the Italian architect Anton (Antonio) Friazin, had a secret passage leading to the Moskva River and a water well. It was later named as the *Tainitskaya* (Secret) Tower.

The circular *Beklemishevskaya* (now *Moskvoretskaya*) Tower was built in 1487 by the Italian architect Marco Friazin. It was named after boyar Beklemishev whose residence was near the construction site. The tower served as a vanguard stronghold to repel enemy attacks.

The circular *Sviblov* Tower (named after boyar Sviblov) was erected at the point of confluence of the Moskva River and its tributary Neglinka. The tower had a water well and a secret passage leading to the river. A water lift was installed in the tower in 1633 supplying water from the well to a reservoir and further into a system of underground piping throughout the Kremlin premises. From that time on, the tower would be referred to as *Vodovzvodnaya* (Water Tower).

The *Blagoveshchenskaya* (Annunciation) Tower was built in 1487-1488 on the stretch of the Moskva River bank between the Tainitskaya and Sviblov towers, taking its name from the miracle-working icon affixed on its façade. The tower had no passage until the *Portomoiny* (Laundry) Gate was constructed in the wall next to it 17th century, used by the Kremlin washerwomen to go to the Moskva River to wash their laundry. In 1831 the Gate was bricked up.

There are another three towers within the interval between the Tainitskaya and Beklemishevskaya Towers: the First and the Second *Bezymyannaya* (Nameless) and the *Petrovskaya* Towers. Originally, the First Bezymyannaya Tower had no passage. During the 15th- 16th centuries it served as a gun-

The Moskvoretskaya Tower.

powder magazine. In the old days, the Second Bezymyannaya Tower had a gate in it. In 1771 both towers were demolished as they interfered with the construction of the Kremlin Palace designed by V.I.Bazhenov, only to be rebuilt after completion of the construction project.

During the 1490s, the construction of the Kremlin fortifications came under the supervision of the Italian architect

The Vodovzvodnaya Tower (left) and the Blagoveshchenskaya Tower.

Pietro Antonio Solari. Working under his guidance was a team of gifted Russian builders.

The construction of the **Borovitskaya** Tower on the western flank of the Kremlin was started in 1490. Provisions and horse fodder were brought into the Kremlin through the Borovitsky Gate. The tower took its name from a dense pine grove (*bor*) that once covered the Kremlin hill.

On the eastern flank of the Kremlin Pietro Antonio Solari built the **Konstantino-Yeleninskaya** Tower. Its function was to protect the settlement around the fortified city. It had rugged detachable firing platform, a drawbridge across the moat and a gate providing access to the Kremlin premises. The tower took its name in the 17th century from the nearby Church of Sts. Konstantin and Yelena.

"A View of Moscow and the Kremlin from the Tainitsky Gate". 1850..
A lithograph by Benois and Obren (from a drawing by Indeitsev).

From right to left: the First and the Second Bezymyannaya Towers, the Petrovskaya Tower, the Moskvoretskaya Tower and the Church of Sts. Konstantin and Yelena.

The Borovitsky Gate of the Moscow Kremlin.
A watercolour painting by I.A.Veis. 1852.

The Konstantino-Yeleninskaya Tower was built on the site of the old *Timofeyevskaya* Tower passed by the Russian troops in 1380 on their way to the Kulikovo Pole. During the first half of the 17th century the Konstantino-Yeleninskaya Tower accommodated the *Razboiny* (Criminal) Tribunal and was later converted into a prison, known as the "torture tower" among common people.

The gateless **Nabatnaya** (Alarm Bell) Tower was erected in 1495 next to the Konstantino-Yeleninskaya Tower. It accommodated the Spassky alarm bell that would be sounded at the sight of the enemy and at times served to give a signal for popular uprisings. The Plague Riot erupted in Moscow in 1771. The rioters sounded the alarm bell to summon people into the Kremlin. After the riot had been suppressed,

The Nabatnaya Tower.

the furious Catherine the Great, unable to track down the person who sounded the alarm, ordered to punish the bell by having its clapper chiselled off.

The "mute" bell remained in the tower for more than 30 years until it was removed and placed in the Arsenal. Today it is kept at the Armoury.

The slim 10-tier *Spasskaya* Tower that took its name from the icons of Saviour of Smolensk and Saviour *Nerukotvorny* (Not of Human Making) has become the easily recognisable symbol of the Moscow cityscape. It was built in 1491 to fortify the Kremlin's eastern flank.

One can still see two white-stone plaques affixed above the tower's gate, with inscriptions in Russian and Latin narrating the story of its construction. These are the oldest surviving commemorative plaques in Moscow. The Spasskaya Tower has double walls constructed of large-size bricks. In between the walls there is a staircase that links together the tower's five tiers. The front gate of the Spasskaya Tower is the Kremlin's main entrance. Back in the 17th century a viaduct-shaped stone bridge led to the gate, protected by a detachable firing platform. Grand princes, tsars and foreign ambassadors would enter the Kremlin through that gate.

The Spassky Gate was regarded as a hallowed place.

The Spassky Gate of the Moscow Kremlin.
A watercolour painting by I.A.Veis. 1852.

The outstanding architect and sculptor V.D.Yermolin worked in the Kremlin during the second half of the 15th century. In 1464 he created the white-stone sculpture of *Saint George the Serpent Warrior* (St.George the Conqueror is the emblem of Moscow). In 1464 it was stationed outside of the entrance gate. Although the sculpture has survived to date, it was severely damaged and is now undergoing restoration.

The Spasskaya Tower clock deserves special mention. In all probability, the tower got its clock shortly after it had been constructed. In 1621, a new clock was ordered from the English clockmaker Christopher Halloway who was serving Tsar Mikhail Fyodorovich on a contract. He directed a team of Russian craftsmen including smith Zhdan, his son and grandson and die-caster Samoilov. To make room for the clock

The Spasskaya Tower clock.

to be installed, engineer Bazhen Ogurtsov added a tent-shaped top to the Spasskaya Tower. That clock was quite different from the one we see today. Its face was divided into 17 segments instead of 12 and its only hand, shaped as a sun ray, stood still against the turnable face.

In the wake of the great fire of 1701 Tsar Peter the Great ordered the "old-fashioned" clock to be replaced by a new one, complete with bell chimes and music. Time did not spare it either...

The modern-day timepiece, designed by the Butenop brothers, was installed in the Spasskaya Tower in 1851-1852. The clock takes up three of the tower's ten tiers. It has 4 faces 6.12 metres in diameter. The length of the hour and the minute hands is 2.97 metres and 3.28 metres, respectively. The height of the digits is 0.72 meters. The overall weight of the clock mechanism is about 25 tons. The clock sends a me-

lodic chime over the Red Square every quarter of an hour. The sound comes from the clock's numerous bells many of which were cast back in the 17th-18th centuries.

Concurrently with the Spasskaya Tower, the *Nikolskaya* (St. Nicholas) Tower was built to Pietro Antonio Solari's design on the Kremlin's north-eastern flank. The Nikolskaya Tower had a gate and was equipped with a detachable firing platform and a drawbridge. It was through that gate that in 1612 the civilian army led by Dmitry Pozharsky and Kozma Minin fought their way into the Kremlin and drove out the Polish invaders.

A gateless square tower was built by Pietro Antonio Solari in 1491 in the stretch between the Spasskaya and the Nikolskaya towers. It remained nameless until the end of the 18th century when, following the construction of the Senate edifice, it was called the *Senatskaya* Tower.

The Nikolsky Gate of the Moscow Kremlin. A watercolour painting by I.A.Veis. 1852.

The third corner tower was constructed in 1492 near the estate of the boyar clan of Sobakins. The Sobakin Tower is the most formidable ingredient of the Kremlin fortifications. Its walls are 4 metres thick. There is a deep draw-well in its basement that would be used as a water source during sieges. The water well has survived to date. After the construction of the Arsenal building in the 18th century, the tower was renamed into the **Corner Arsenalnaya** Tower. The **Middle Arsenalnaya** Tower was built in 1493-95 next to the Corner

Arsenalnaya Tower on the site of a corner tower that stood there back in the times of Dmitry Donskoy.

The tallest of all the Kremlin towers – the *Troitskaya* (Trinity) Tower – was built in 1495. It took its name in 1658 from the nearby Troitsky (Trinity) monastery. The Troitskaya Tower came second in the order of importance among the Kremlin towers. Its gate gave access to the Patriarch's Palace and to the tsarinas' and tsarevnas' quarters.

The *Kutafya* Tower was constructed in 1516 to safeguard access routes leading to the Troitskaya Tower. The Neglinka River was spanned with a stone bridge that linked the two towers together. The word "Kutafya" means "clumsy". The tower presented a formidable obstacle to attackers. Completely encircled by the river, it could only be entered through a suspension bridge. The Kutafya Tower is the only surviving ingredient of the Kremlin's outer ring of fortifications.

The construction of a string of staunch towers along the swampy banks of the Neglinka River was completed by 1495. The gateless *Kolymazhnaya* Tower was built to the south of the Troitskaya Tower, taking its name from the nearby *Kolymazhny Dvor* (Carriage Yard). In the 19th century when the Commandant of Moscow settled at the nearby Poteshny Palace it was renamed into **Komendantskaya** (Commandant's) Tower.

The *Konyushennaya* (Stables) Tower was built in between the Borovitskaya and the Komendantskaya towers close to the tsar's stables. In 1851, following the construction of the Armoury, it was renamed into **Oruzheinaya** (Armoury) Tower.

The *Tsarskaya* (Tsar's) Tower that sits on top of the Kremlin wall was built much later in 1680. This unusual tent-like structure resting on jug-shaped pillars look more like a miniature fairytale palace than a detail of citadel fortifications. A legend has it that a wooden tower stood there in the old days, from where Tsar Ivan the Terrible watched the events taking place in the Red Square.

The Kremlin wall and the towers were constructed according to the best contemporary standards of military fortifications engineering.

The multi-tier towers were provided with several rows of embrasures for rifle and canon fire. The top tier had *machicolations* – slanting embrasures which made it possible to discharge missiles at assailants at very foot of the towers.

Special emphasis was placed on the defensive capabilities of the Kremlin's five gate towers. They were provided with barbicans, detachable firing platforms, drawbridges and portcullis. In the event that the attackers were able to break through the outer fortifications, bridge and gate, an iron grating would be lowered in the gateway behind them, locking them in a trap. Although the portcullis did not survive to date, one can still see the grooves in the Borovistky gateway between which they were lowered in the old days.

A water-filled moat designed by Alevisio Friazin (*Alevisio's moat*) 32 metres wide and 12 metres deep was dug on the Red Square flank in 1508-1516 in the time of Prince Vassily III with the purpose of strengthening the Kremlin defences. It linked together the Moskva River (on the south) and the Neglinka River (on the south-west).

The Moscow fire of 1812.
I.K. Aivazovsky.

The Kremlin was thus transformed into an insular fortress reliably protected from every side. The moat was levelled in 1801.

The defences of the Kremlin citadel improved century after century. The design of the fortifications changed to keep pace with the development of the obsidional machinery.

According to Russian chroniclers, large-scale construction was resumed on the Kremlin premises in the 1620s. During 1624-1685 all the Kremlin towers with the exception of the Nikolskaya Tower were topped with tent-like tile roofs which gave a picturesque touch to the citadel's austere lineament and accentuated the towers' skyward stature. According to the renowned historian I. Ye. Zabelin, *"the construction of the roofs did nothing to strengthen the Kremlin fortifications but it did impart a different kind of an eternal strength to it, through an artistic expression of the poesy and spirit of pre-Petrine Rus"*.

The emblem of Russia – the double-headed eagle – was mounted on top of the Spasskaya Tower during the 1650s and later on the tallest towers: the Nikolskaya, the Troitskaya and the Borovistkaya towers.

The 1812 war with France inflicted immeasurable damage on the city of Moscow and the Kremlin. The Vodovzvodnaya, the First Bezymyannaya and the Petrovskaya towers were blown into heaps of stone debris; the tent roof of the Borovitskaya Tower was nearly halved and the Nikolskaya Tower was almost completely destroyed. Severe damage was sustained by the Corner Arsenalnaya Tower and the Kremlin wall.

The work to repair the damage was carried out during 1817-1822 under the

Inside the Kremlin wall.

supervision of the outstanding Russian architect O.I. Bove.

The Moscow Kremlin had from times immemorial been the hub of the Russian statehood and the residence of the Russian tsars and the patriarchs of the Russian Orthodox Church. Although early in the 18th century Peter the Great ordered the Russian capital to be relocated to St. Petersburg, the coronation of Russian emperors would traditionally be held in Moscow.

In 1918 when Moscow regained the status of the capital city, the Soviet government and the supreme bodies of state power moved into the Kremlin.

Over time, the appearance of the Kremlin was changed to suit the ruling ideology. In 1935-1937 the double-headed eagles on the towers were replaced with five-point stars.

In 1945-1946 the design of the stars underwent major alterations. The new stars were made of three-ply ruby glass plates fitted into stainless steel frames capable of withstanding maximum wind pressure. The metallic parts were coated with a layer of gold 50 microns thick.

The Kremlin stars are internally illuminated 24 hours a day by lamps of 3,700 to 5,000 Watts, depending on the size of a particular star. There are special fans that serve to cool down the heat emanated by the lamps.

The star rays extend from 3 to 3.75 metres and the weight of the stars varies from 1 to 1.5 tons. Mounted on bearings, the stars are capable of turning albeit in a light breeze.

In the post-revolutionary period restoration work in the Kremlin was carried out on a continuous basis. In our time, the restoration specialists employ the leading-edge technology and scientific recommendations.

Like a necklace, the wall and the towers of the Kremlin engirdle the palaces and the cathedrals rising from the Borovitsky hill, blending them all into a single architectural ensemble. The position of the Kremlin's major edifices had been well established by the end of the 14th century. By the 17th century, the Kremlin had evolved into a city complete with **squares, streets** and side lanes.

In the middle of the Kremlin there are two old squares – the *Cathedral* and the *Ivanovskaya* squares.

Leading to these squares was the Kremlin's main artery – the *Spasskaya* Street.

The *Troitskaya* and the *Nikolskaya* (St.Nicholas) streets ran from the Troitskaya and the Nikolskaya towers, repeating the pattern of old mud roads. The *Zhitnaya* and the *Borovitskaya* streets can be seen in the south-western segment of the Kremlin on the old maps and drawings.

Located within the confines of the *Great Tsar's Courtyard* where the edifices of the Great Kremlin Palace and the Armoury were erected in the 19th century, was the *Dvortsovaya* (Palatial) or *Imperatorskaya* (Imperatorial) Square. The *Troitsky podvorie* (now *Troitskaya* Square), neighbouring the Great Tsar's Courtyard, accommodated the holdings of the high-placed boyars and their relatives.

The *Dvortsovaya* Street (former *Komendantskaya* St.) linked the Troitskaya Square to the Dvortsovaya Square.

There is also the *Senatskaya* (Senate) Square in the Kremlin, which has retained its early 19th century appearance. The Cathedral Square is the aesthetic, historical and planning centre of the Kremlin. The old documents refer to it simply as *"the square"* or *"the courtyard between the cathedrals and the Kremlin Palace"*. Traditionally, it was where the monarchs met foreign ambassadors and where ceremonial processions passed on their way to the Cathedral of the Assumption during coronations and festal liturgies. The stone pavement of the square had a pathway laid with granite slabs – the so-called *Tsar's pathway* – that ran from the southern entrance of the Cathedral of the Assumption to the Red Porch of the Kremlin Palace.

The Cathedral Square acquired its present-day appearance in the late 15th – early 16th centuries after the Kremlin's principal cathedrals and churches had been constructed on its premises.

UNDER THE AUSPICES OF GOLDEN DOMES

Encircling the Cathedral Square are outstanding specimens of old Russian architecture: cathedrals and churches, the Belfry of Ivan the Great and the Bell Tower , the Facets Palace, the Patriarch's Palace.

The *Cathedral of the Assumption* was built as the principal church of the Russian state. It was designed by the architect Aristotle Fioravanti during 1475-1479.

The cathedral rises on the northern side of the square where once stood the Kremlin's oldest sanctuary composed of a wooden church and a burial ground. In 1326, Metropolitan Peter ordered the metropolitan quarters to be relocated from Vladimir to Moscow. Concurrently, Prince Ivan Kalita launched the construction of the Cathedral of the Assumption chosen by Metropolitan Peter as the burial place for himself.

In 1472, the foundation of the new cathedral was laid in place of the old dilapidated edifice. The construction project was supervised by a tandem of Moscow architects, Krivtsov and Myshkin. Two years later, however, the nearly complete building suddenly collapsed. To construct a new cathedral the Grand Prince Ivan III requested the services of the renowned Italian architect and engineer Aristotle Fioravanti of Bologna. The Moscow princes sought to establish their supremacy over the rest of the Russian principalities and prove their right to directly succeed to the powers of the grand princes of Vladimir, the ancient capital city of the north-eastern Rus. With that in mind, Fioravanti was told to build a cathedral that would be modelled after the Cathedral of the Assumption in Vladimir, a gem of early Russian architecture. The construction took four years. The newly built cathedral was consecrated in 1479.

The cathedral's architectural design represents a revised version of the traditional Russian cross-vaulted design of church edifices. The Cathedral of the Assumption is built of white limestone as a six-pillar, five-dome structure. The portals serving as gala entrances are girdled with arcs and decorated with murals. The grandeur of the cathedral's appearance comes from its monolithic design and austere proportions.

The outstanding architect was able to make the entire edifice look *"as if it were carved from a solid rock"*, as a contemporary chronicler would have it.

The Cathedral of the Assumption surpassed all the earlier churches both in

The Cathedral of the Assumption.

size and splendour of its interior. The cathedral's interior is spaceous and well-lit, which is quite unusual for Russian medieval churches. Seen from inside, it looks like a grand ceremonial hall. Its high vaulted ceiling traditionally rests on six pillars, two of which rise from the altar and are square in cross-section.

The other four pillars located in the main part of the cathedral are circular, which makes the interior easily observable in every direction. The Italian architect dispensed with traditional church choir gallery and chose not to accentuate the interior's spatial centre, which all the more makes it look like a secular hall.

The interior of the Cathedral of the Assumption.

The cathedral, purported to play an important role in the country's life, was adorned painstakingly. Two years after its construction the far-famed painter Dionysius and his assistants created a three-tier iconostasis. Presumably, the great artist himself painted several frescoes (a *fresco* is a painting on freshly spread moist lime plaster with water-based pigments). Some fragments of the oldest 15th century frescoes can still be seen in the altar and on the stone

Frescoes on the southern wall.

altar barrier. The cathedral's walls were painted with frescoes in the early 16th century in the time of Vassily Ivanovich, son of Prince Ivan III. In the 17th century the frescoes were chipped off. The walls were repainted in 1642-1643 in the time of Tsar Mikhail Fyodorovich. The work was performed by some 150 skilled painters from Moscow and other Russian cities led by the court icon painters Ivan and Boris Paiseins. The 16th century themes and the arrangement of paintings, repeated in the course of the renovation, were conceived as a model to be followed in painting the interiors of other cathedrals. This explains the strict observance of the overall canonical archetype of the wall paintings. The most significant themes involving Christ, evangelists, forefathers and prophets were painted inside the domes and on the vaulted ceilings which, according to the Christian tradition, are the most important parts of the interior. The pillars that support the vaults bear the images of 135 martyrs. The cathedral's wall paintings tell the life story of the Virgin and illustrate "The Acathistos" – a hymn of worship of the Virgin.

In keeping with tradition, the cathedral's western wall accommodates "The Last Judgement", a composition of impressive proportions exploring the theme of reward or punishment for righteous or sinful life in the inevitable hereafter.

The magnificent ensemble of the murals in the Cathedral of the Assumption pieces together 249 thematic compositions and 2,066 individual characters. Tier by tier, the frescoes engirdle the walls of the cathedral, as if narrating the story in strict sequence. The murals and the inspiring architecture create an inimitable sensation of spiritual exaltation and everlasting beauty.

A new 16-metre iconostasis in a silver framework was made for the cathedral in 1653 at the of order of Patriarch Nikon. It consisted of 69 icons arranged in four tiers: deeisis, festal, prophets' and forefathers'. The iconostasis of the Cathedral of the Assumption is departs from the Russian iconostasis tradition because like in Greek churches its deesis tier icons represent the "apostolic row" – the images of the twelve apostles praying to Christ, preceded by the Virgin, John the Baptist and the Archangels.

In 17th century the lower tier icons were also arranged according to the Greek standard.

The Greek icon "The Saviour on the Throne" (its wooden base is dated at 11th century) was positioned at the most distinguished place to the right of the Tsar's Doors. According to the canon, the cathedral's dedicated icon – "The Assumption of the Virgin" (15th century) – was positioned next on the right. The encased icon of "The Virgin of Vladimir" (1514) could be seen to the left of the Tsar's Doors. It replaced the 12th century version of "The Virgin of Vladimir", a far-famed creation of a Greek artist. At present, the older icon is on display at the Tretyakov Art Gallery.

Century after century, Russia's sacred objects – best icons and applied art articles – were brought to the Cathedral of the Assumption. The cathedral holds a magnificent collection of old icons, including unique masterpieces such as "Saint George" (12th century) with later addition (middle of the 14th century) of the image of "The Virgin of Hodegetria", "The Saviour of the Fiery Eye" (middle of the 14th century), "The Virgin of Vladimir" (15th century).

Quite a few Greek and Balkanic painters worked in Russia in the late 14th – early 15th centuries. Thus, the icon "Crucifixion" at the Cathedral of the Assumption was apparently painted by a Greek artist and the icon "Sts. Peter and Paul" shows Byzantine influence.

The icon of the Virgin of Vladimir.
Moscow. 1514.

Kept at the Cathedral is a collection of icons painted in the late 15th – early 16th centuries at the time when the independent state of Russia was taking shape. These include: "Metropolitan Peter and Scenes from His Life", "All Creation Rejoices in Thee", "Apocalypse" and "The Church Militant".

As early as the 15th century the Cathedral had pews for Metropolitans. The tsar's pew known as the *Throne of Monomachus* was made for Ivan the Terrible in 1551, four years after his coronation. It is a unique specimen of decorative wood carving (linden and walnut). Carved on the throne's side panels are scenes of Vladimir Monomachus receiving the insignia of royal power from the Byzantine emperor Constantine Monomachus.

The upper portion of the throne's canopy is adorned with *kokoshniki* resembling tiaras covered with delicately carved open-worked ornament, while the four legs are shaped as some fantastic creatures symbolising royal powers.

In the early days the projecting parts of the carved ornaments were gilded and the flat background was painted in gold, blue and red pigments.

In the 17th century, the tsarina's carved wooden pew was stationed by the north-west pillar in front of the iconostasis. It was brought there from the domestic chapel for Maria Ilyinichna Miloslavsky, the first spouse of Tsar Alexei Mikhailovich.

In the south-western part of the cathedral there is a tent-shaped shrine, cast of bronze in 1624 by Dmitry Sverchkov and designed for keeping sacred objects. Kept in a golden casket on the communion table was one of the most precious Christian relics – a fragment of the robe worn by Christ, which had been sent to Tsar Mikhail Fydorovich by the Persian Shah Abbas I as a gift. At present, the shrine accommodates a reliquary holding the remains of Patriarch Hermogen (canonised in 1913), an antagonist of the Polish invasion in the early 17th century. The reliquary

was placed in the shrine during the restoration of the cathedral timed for the celebrations of the 300th anniversary of the Romanov dynasty.

An admirable item of the cathedral's interior is the massive chandelier designed by A.Gedlung and weighing 328 kg. It was cast from silverware recaptured by the Cossacks from the retreating Napoleonic army in 1812.

The Cathedral of the Assumption was built to host official ceremonies and rites of national significance including designations of grand dukes, coronations of tsars and later, of emperors, as well as ordainments of of the Russian Orthodox Church primates.

Buried inside the cathedral were Russian metropolitans and patriarchs of the 14th – 17th centuries. Their remains lie in the graves beneath the cathedral floor with white tombstones above. The metal encasements of the tombstones were made in the early 20th century by craftsmen of the Khlebnikov firm.

Special note should be made of the entombment of the primate of the Russian Orthodox Church Metropolitan Peter, who had transferred the Metropolitan pulpit from Vladimir to Moscow and after his death was declared an officially recognised saint.

The grave of Metropolitan Kiprian, a diplomat and educator, is in the south-western part of the cathedral. It was during his tenure that the icon of "The Virgin of Vladimir" was brought from Vladimir to Moscow *"to safeguard against the armies of the Horde King Temir-Aksak"* (Tamerlane).

Metropolitan Fothium, buried next to him was also canonised. During 1408-1431 he was the head of the Russian Orthodox Church. Till 1918, the Ca-

The bronze tent-shaped shrine. Moscow. 1624.

thedral of the Assumption was the principal church in Russia. In 1990, religious services were resumed in the cathedral. On great church holidays the service would be conducted by the Patriarch of Moscow and All Russia. In our time, it is also one of the most visited Kremlin museums.

The *Cathedral of the Annunciation*, a gem of old Russian architecture, stands in the southern part of the Cathedral Square. It was a domestic church of grand princes and tsars and was designed to host family events (weddings, christening of infants, etc.). Part of the tsar's personal quarters, the cathedral was originally linked with passages to the tsar's palace and the Archangel Cathedral.

The history of the Cathedral of the Annunciation dates back many centuries. The remains of the old substructure found by archaeologists show that a stone church of the Annunciation stood there at the end of the 14th century. In 1416, another church – of bigger proportions — was built on its extant basement.

The slender, soaring Cathedral of the Annunciation was built in 1484-1489 by craftsmen from Pskov in place of the dilapidated church of the early 15th century. Originally, the cathedral had three domes and was encircled by open galleries.

The cathedral acquired its present-day appearance during the reign of Ivan the Terrible in the second half of the 16th century when it was re-designed through the addition of single-domed chapels at all the four corners; also, two ornamental domes were constructed on the western side of the cathedral increasing the overall number of domes to nine. The domes and the roofs were gilded. A legend links the rebuilding of the porch to the fourth marriage of Ivan the Terrible who was put under a penance and by the Christian rules could not attend services inside the cathedral but had to stand on the porch. As a matter of fact, the existing porch is a surviving portion of the cathedral

built in 1489. It provided passage from the tsar's palace to the administrative building located between the Archangel Cathedral and the Cathedral of the Annunciation, as well as to the Archangel Cathedral and the palatial gardens.

In the 16th century, the portals of the cathedral's main edifice were redesigned by Italian stone-carvers. The tall two-leaved doors were faced with copper sheets inlaid with gold and showing biblical scenes. The interior of the Cathedral of the Annunciation is relatively small and it is made even smaller by the choir gallery located in its western part. The cathedral's floor made from pieces of jasper-agate of various shades is particularly impressive.

The cathedral's wall paintings were first mentioned by chroniclers in 1508. The frescoes were painted by Theodosius, son of the famous icon painter Dionysius. The fire of 1547, sorrowfully cited by Russian chroniclers, destroyed most of the wall paintings. The cathedral walls were repainted in 1547-1551. During the 17th – 19th centuries, the frescoes were repeatedly renovated and overpainted with oil paints.

The Cathedral of the Annunciation is one of the few monuments of old Russian architecture preserving original 16th century murals created by a succession of Russian painters.

The vaulted gallery ceiling harbours the "Tree of Jesus", a composition showing the family tree of Christ including not only his progenitors but also his disciples – the apostles. It also includes images of ancient philosophers, historians and poets: Homer, Virgil, Plato, Plutarch, seen as prophesiers of Christ. The "Tree" composi-

The Cathedral of the Annunciation.

tion symbolises the prehistory and history of Christianity. Themes from the "Apocalypse" – an early Christian writing about the imminent end of humankind and the Final Judgement – occupy a prominent place among other wall paintings in the central portion of the cathedral.

The copper-plated doors. The 16ᵗʰ–17ᵗʰ centuries.

The pillars of the cathedral are decorated with stylised portraits of Byzantine Emperor Constantine (who raised Christianity to the status of official religion), his mother Yelena, the Kievan Princess Olga and Prince Vladimir who ordered Christian conversion of Russia.

The iconostasis of the Cathedral of the Annunciation.

The pillars opposite them bear the images of martyr warriors St. George and Dmitry Solunsky and the first Russian saints – princes Boris and Gleb. The gallery of righteous men also includes Russian princes: Vladimir Monomachus, Alexander Nevsky, Ivan Kalita, Dmitry Donskoy, Vassily I.

The icon of Annunciation.
Andrei Rublev (?). 1450(?).

The cathedral's wall paintings echo the state doctrine that proclaimed Moscow a "Third Rome" and legitimised the Moscow tsars' claim that their powers were directly succeeded from Byzantine emperors and the Roman Emperor Augustus. The paintings on the cathedral's pillars served to emphasise the succession of the Moscow grand princes' powers from the Kievan princes and the Byzantine emperors.

A multi-tier iconostasis was an important ingredient of any old Russian church. The iconostasis of the Cathedral of the Annunciation, unique in its artistic value, collates icons painted by different artists and at various times within the 14th century – 19th century span.

The icons of the *deesis* and the *festal* tiers, the most important tiers of the iconostasis, are the most enigmatic works of old Russian art. They are attributed to three great old Russian painters: Theophanus the Greek, Prokhor s Gorodtsa and Andrei Rublev. Although the outstanding elegance of forms, the richness of colours and unique painting techniques suggest that they were created by great artists, the authorship of the icons remains unidentified.

In the middle of the 16th century, craftsmen from Pskov painted the icons of the *prophets'* tier of the iconostasis. The uppermost tier – the *forefathers'*, consists of small icons painted in the 16th and 19th centuries and shaped like *kokoshniki*. The icons of the lowermost, local saints' tier, painted by Russian and Byzantine artists, are dated back to the 14th – early 18th centuries. A graceful encasement of gilded copper with enamelled ornament was made for the iconostasis in the 19th century. At present, a collection of icons is displayed in the cathedral's southern gallery, many of which originally belonged to the side chapels.

During the 15th – 17th centuries the cathedral's basement housed the grand princes' and later on, the tsar's treasury. Today, it is the site of the permanent exhibition *"The Archaeology of the Moscow Kremlin"* that describes the history of the earliest settlement on the Borovitsky Hill.

A legend has it that back in the 13th century a wooden church stood near the hill's southern slope. It was built by Mikhail Khrabry (Courageous), Alexander Nevsky's brother, to commemorate his guardian, Archangel Mikhail. In the time of Prince Ivan Kalita it was replaced with a white stone church, the largest in the Kremlin, according to the chroniclers. Prince Ivan Kalita was the first to be buried on its premises.

In 1505-1508, in the time of Grand Prince Ivan III, the time-worn edifice was demolished to be replaced with a cathedral. Designed by the Italian architect Alevisio Novy, it has survived to date. The cathedral bearing the name of Archangel Mikhail, the guardian of princes and Russian warriors, was to become the sepulcher of grand princes.

The Venetian architect imparted some contemporary traits of the Renaissance palatial architecture to the edifice of the **Archangel Cathedral**: its façades are decorated with pilasters complete with ornate Corinthian capitals, set apart by decorative arches; the carved white stone gables of each façade section are shaped like semicircular seashells.

The cathedral's northern and the western portals are richly decorated with carved ornaments. The main entrance on the western side forms a wide niche (loggia). The southern façade, overlooking the Moskva River, was redesigned at the end of the 18th century when architect Bazhenov reinforced the cathedral with *buttresses*. By its exterior, the cathedral looks more like a secular edifice that a building consecrated to worship.

The cathedral's interior is somewhat cramped by thick square pillars that divide the building into three *naves*. The cathedral is illuminated by magnificent chandeliers specially manufac-

The Archangel Cathedral.

tured for it by Moscow craftsmen in the late 17th – early 18th centuries.

For the first time, the interior of the cathedral was painted with frescoes in the second half of the 16th century in the time of Tsar Ivan the Terrible. Fragments of the frescoes can still be seen in the altar area. During 1652-1666, in the time of Tsar Alexei Mikhailovich, the interior of the cathedral was repainted by a large team of artists from various Russian cities. Simon Ushakov, a famous icon painter in charge of the Armoury's icon-painting shop, personally selected applicants for the job. The 17th century frescoes fully repro-

The interior of the Archangel Cathedral.

duced the concept and the themes of the previous paintings.

The 17th century wall paintings were reopened for viewing in the 1960s after restoration. The cathedral's frescoes are remarkable for exquisite drawing techniques, cheerful colour pattern, sophistication and wealth of content.

Alongside traditional biblical scenes the frescoes reflect important political ideas prevalent in the time of Tsar Ivan the Terrible. It is not without reason that painted next to the scenes from the "Final Judgement" on the western wall of the cathedral is the composition "The Symbol of Faith", a compact il-

The Tsar's Doors. 1679-1681.

lustration of the fundamentals of Christianity. Presumably, it was painted in the cathedral in connection with the struggle against heretical teachings in the second half of the 16th century for the consolidation of unshakeable dogmas of Orthodox Christianity. The

paintings on the southern and northern walls, describing the exploits of Archangel Mikhail, present a purposeful exploration of a heroic theme reflecting real-life events that occurred during the reign of Ivan the Terrible. The battle scenes shown in the frescoes

THE MOSCOW KREMLIN

The princes of the Moscow dynasty.
Frescoes on the southern wall. 1652-1666.

are associated with the century-long struggle of Rus against the Mongol-Tatar oppression, culminating in the defeat of the Golden Horde and the incorporation of the Kazan and the Astrakhan khanates into the Russian state.

A remarkable point about the cathedral's frescoes is that the pillars and the walls lowermost tier contain over 60 images of real historical personalities, making up an improvised portrait gallery of Moscow princes and their ancestors, from Grand Prince Vladimir onwards.

The portraits are arranged according to a specific pattern. The images of Moscow dynasty princes, buried in the cathedral, occupy the lower tier of the southern, northern and western walls. The painted figures form some sort of a solemn procession moving towards the altar. The circular halos above their heads incorporate the images of saints who bless them to proceed. The long succession of figures is no way monotonous. Every one of them has individual traits: a different body movement, a different turn of the head, a different position of the hands. Every one of them is clad in a different attire of ornamented fabric, decorated with precious stones and furs. The symbolic disks of light around their heads serve to accentuate their "God-chosen" status, even though none of them was

Icon of Archangel Mikhail with Deeds. Detail of the centre piece. Moscow. The late 14ᵗʰ – early 15ᵗʰ centuries.

declared a saint with the exception of Dmitry Donskoy, canonised in 1989. The first iconostasis of the Archangel Cathedral made up with 16ᵗʰ century icons has not survived to date. In 1679-1681, a new 4-tier iconostasis was made. The rich ornamentation of its carved (linden wood) gilded framework is consistent with the tradition of the Moscow baroque style that domi-nated the Russian art at the end of the 17ᵗʰ century. The icons were painted by the court artists under the supervision of the famous icon-painter Fyodor Zubov.

The cathedral's oldest icon is "Archangel Mikhail with Deeds", created by an unknown artist of the late 14ᵗʰ century. A legend has it that the icon was painted at the order from Grand Princess Yevdokia, the widow of Dmitry Donskoy, as a homage to her deceased husband. The heroic image of Archangel Mikhail, the patron of Russian soldiers, incorporates the attributes of an ideal warrior.

The Archangel Cathedral served as a dynasty sepulchre right until Peter the Great relocated the Russian capital to Saint Petersburg where monarchs would be buried thereupon. The only exception was made for Peter II who died of smallpox in Moscow in 1730. The deceased dignitaries were buried under the cathedral's floor. They lie beneath 46 white stone entombments, decorated with carved ornaments and bearing inscriptions made in the first half of the 17th century.

The remains of the Moscow grand princes lie buried by the cathedral's southern wall. Along the western wall are the graves of appanage princes, while those of disgraced princes are by the northern wall.

Tsar Ivan the Terrible and his two sons are buried at the segregated place in the altar behind the iconostasis. In the middle of the cathedral, under a carved white stone canopy and behind a 17th century openwork bronze grille is the tomb of Tsarevich Dmitry, the youngest son of Ivan the Terrible, who died in Uglich in 1591. He was canonised in 1605 and in 1606 his remains were transferred to Moscow. The epitaph on his tombstone reads, *"Truth rests in Eternity, devoid of sorrow as long as Glory reigns the Earth"*. The middle part of the cathedral accommodates the tombs of the first tsars of the Romanov dynasty.

At the beginning of the 20th century, in commemoration of the 300th anniversary of the Romanov dynasty, the tombs were enclosed in copper-and-glass encasements inscribed with the names of the deceased and the dates of their demise.

In the old days, Moscow princes would visit the Archangel Cathedral on the eve of a military campaign to pay tribute to their ancestors and to glorify "the courage and valor of the Russian warriors".

At present, the Archangel Cathedral of Kremlin serves as a museum housing the ancient tombs and providing a fine example of medieval décor. Church services are also held there.

The slender single-domed **Church of the Deposition of the Robe** stands in the Cathedral Square between the Cathedral of the Assumption and the Facets Palace. It used to be a domestic church of Russian metropolitans but after 1589, when patriarchate was instituted, it became a church of Russian patriarchs. Like any other Kremlin church, it was built in place of an older church of the same name.

According to historical records for the year 1450, *"Metropolitan Jonah laid the foundation stone of the Church of the Deposition of the Robe"*. The great fire of 1473 destroyed the original church together with metropolitan's quarters. A new church was built on the same site and it is the one we can see today. Constructed from 1484 to 1485 by craftsmen from Pskov, it was dedicated to a holiday, first celebrated in Byzantium in the 15th century, when a great relic – the Virgin's robe – was brought to Constantinople from Palestine. In Rus, the robe was regarded as miracle-working shrine capable of keeping enemies away.

The Church of the Deposition of the Robe is a comparatively small edifice.

*The Church
of the Deposition of the Robe.*

Standing on an elevated substructure it catches the eye by the elegance of design and façade decoration. Especially attractive is the twin terra-cotta frieze engirdling three flanks of the building. The décor of the cupola drum is typical of the Pskov-style architecture. Inside, the church looks snug and homely. Slim, four-sided pillars support the vaulted arches that hold the soaring dome.

The interior of the church is decorated with frescoes painted in 1644 by Sidor Pospeyev, Ivan Borisov and Semyon Abramov. Thematically, the frescoes explore the theme of the Virgin. "The Life of the Virgin" narrates the story of her childhood, youth and ascent to heaven. Portrayed on the southern wall of the church is the scene of the miraculous rescue of Constantinople from enemy siege after the patriarch had dipped the Virgin's robe into the waters of the bay. The small size of the church predetermined the scale of the wall paintings that look more like icons. The paintings take up the entire perimeter of the walls and are arranged horizontally in five tiers. Painted below are white ornamented draperies. This tradition was imported from Byzantium where the lowermost portions of church walls were draped with pieces of cloth, later replaced with painted imitations.

The frescoes on the pillars are also noteworthy: the southern pillar is painted with illustrations of the Moscow tsar family tree, while the northern pillar bears the images of Moscow metropolitans, predecessors of the Russian patriarchs.

The frescoes of the church of patriarchs extol the authority of the church and its alliance with the powers of the Moscow princes safeguarded by the Virgin.

The colourful frescoes provide a matching background for the iconostasis, created in 1627 to the order of Patriarch Filaret by Nazary Istomin-Savin, one of the best icon-painters of

The Great Accession.
Fresco. 1644.

the early 17th century. He painted the three upper tiers of the iconostasis and two icons in the lower tier to the left of the Tsar's Doors: "The Trinity" and "The Virgin with Child"

The artistic skills of the famous painter are really striking: his drawing techniques are calligraphically precise and truly virtuosic. The use of pure red and white pigments against a soft colour scheme produces a festive effect, further heightened by the silver icon frames. The lower, local saints' tier is made up with icons painted in the 16th – 17th centuries.

Positioned on both sides of the Tsar's Doors are the dedicated icons: "The Deposition of the Virgin's Robe", "The Virgin of Tikhvin", "The Trinity" by Nazary Istomin, and the icon of the Virgin portrayed full-length. The wall frescoes perfectly match the iconostasis forming an unbroken pictorial ensemble.

Because a new domestic church was constructed for Patriarch Nikon in the middle of the 17th century, the Church of the Deposition of the Robe was attached to the Terem Palace and linked to it with a roofed passage.

At present, the north gallery of the church houses a small exhibition of wooden sculptures of the 15th – 17th centuries, including large carved icons

Statue of St. Nicholas of Mozhaisk. The 17ᵗʰ century.

and small folded icons used by travellers. The icons were crafted in Novgorod, Rostov Veliky and other northern Russian cities famous for their wood carving traditions. Exemplary of the high level of craftsmanship of the wood carvers is the image of Metropolitan Jonah made for his tomb at the Cathedral of the Assumption, and the monumental statue of St. George, created in the late 14ᵗʰ – early 15ᵗʰ centuries.

Another fine example is the 17ᵗʰ century statue of St. Nicholas of Mozhaisk, a model of the Mozhaisk fortress in his left hand and a sword — to ward off the enemies — in his right hand. Old Russian wooden sculptures reveal a distinct relationship with original folk art. Regrettably, very few such works have survived to date. It is therefore all the more exciting to see them on display in the Church of the Deposi-

tion of the Robe – a remarkable monument of old Russian culture.

The architectural ensemble of the Cathedral Square is consummated on its north side by the edifice of the **Patriarch's Palace** complete with the five-domed **Church of the Twelve Apostles**. As early as the first decades of the 14ᵗʰ century, the Metropolitan quarters stood on that spot. The earliest stone building was constructed there in 1450. *"Metropolitan Jonah laid the foundation of a stone residence in his courtyard"*, wrote a contemporary chronicler.

Over centuries the metropolitan residence was frequently destroyed by fires and rebuilt.

A considerable period in the history of the Palace is associated with Patriarch Nikon(1605-1681). In 1653 he ordered a major overhaul of his residence by a team of best architects, painters, gold-

Icon of The Deposition of the Virgin's Robe. First half of the 17ᵗʰ century.

The Patriarch's Palace
and the Church of the Twelve Apostles.

smiths and stone-carvers. Within two years the palace of the top church hierarch was in no way inferior to the tsar's residence in terms of its size, architectural design and richly decorated interior. It is known that Patriarch Nikon was a staunch advocate of his own political doctrine of *"Priesthood over Tsardom"*.

In 1721 when Peter the Great abolished patriarchate and dissolved the Holy Synod, the Patriarch Palace became the seat of the Moscow Governing Synod. The palace edifice and the adjoining domestic Church of the Twelve Apostles represent a one-piece architectural ensemble. The church stands on elevated arches with passages. The white stone exterior of the Patriarch's Palace echoes that of other architectural monuments grouped within the Cathedral Square.

The palace's numerous chambers were linked together with vestibules and passages. In keeping with the tradition, the ground floor was used for household services; the first floor accommodated the offices and the domestic chapel and the second was taken up by the Patriarch's personal quarters.

The *Krestovaya Palata* (The Hall of the Cross) is the principal official hall in the palace. It was where the patriarch received the tsar and foreign ambassadors and where church councils (sobors) and feasts were held. In 1763, the

*Exhibits on display
in Krestovaya Palata.*

hall was renamed into the Chrism Chamber, after a stove for making chrism was built there. The ritual of chrism-making would be performed there until 1918.

The hall taking up the area of 280 square metres has a vaulted ceiling with no supporting pillars and is remarkable for its innovative architectural design and rich interior. Originally, the floor of the hall was laid with beautiful green tiles.

From 1963 on, the Patriarch's Palace houses the *Museum of Applied Art and Life Style of 17th century Russia* displaying selected items from the collections of the Armoury and the Kremlin cathedrals. Exhibited here are scores of household articles such as old Russian tableware, silver and gold items imported from Oriental and Western countries, jewelry collections of tabletop clocks and pocket watches, accessories from the tsar's ceremonial equipage gear and hunting tackle.

Representative of the art and life style of the 17th century, the exhibits give viewers a better idea of the old Russia's cultural legacy and traditions.

The articles showcased in the smaller vestibule tell the story of how the Metropolitan and then the Patriarchal residence came into being on the Kremlin premises. Displayed in the front vestibule are both religious and household articles owned by the 17th century Rus-

Patriarch Nikon's staff and cowl.

sian church hierarchs: a *sakkos*, a home *caftan* and a *klobuk* of Patriarch Nikon; a *bratina* of Patriarch Filaret; a bratina and a goblet of Patriarch Joseph alongside a silver staff decorated with precious stones.

The magnificence and the ostentatious richness of these articles are indicative of the characteristic trend of that period towards the similarity of the official attributes used by the rivalling clerical and the secular powers.

Two other chambers retaining their original architectural design provide an idea of the everyday life style of wealthy Moscow residents. These two rather small rooms have low vaulted ceilings and narrow windows with panes made of mica. In the past they must have looked quite cheerful with walls clad in bright-coloured fabric, embossed gilded leather and imported textiles and the floor covered with coloured felt. Stoves were decorated with multicoloured glazed clay tiles. Icons played a prominent role in the interior. Icons would be positioned in the best decorated corner of the room. Habitually, these chambers would be furnished with wide benches covered with colourful spreads. Household utensils and tableware were stored in chests.

With the changes in the antiquated lifestyle in the second half of the 17th century came changes in the interior

*Exhibition
in a living chamber.*

of living apartments. According to a contemporary witness, those became *"a mix of the old and new styles"*. Traditional Russian furniture co-existed with a Dutch dresser and a German cupboard; icons would be placed next to portraits of Tsar Alexei Mikhailovich and courtier P.I.Potemkin.

It is worth while observing the handwritten and printed books of the 17th century (the 1693 "ABC Book" by Karion Istomin, "A Medicine for the Soul", "The Grammar Book" and "The Gospel"). The interior of wealthy people's 17th century living apartment was reconstructed from documented evidence and genuine articles dating back to that period.

The refectory of the Patriarch's Palace now houses a collection of old Russian decorative and ornamental gold-stitch embroidery. Articles produced by that original techniques were used for a wide variety of purposes: as covers for church vessels and spreads for the tombs of saints and altar cloths for icons. All those items were once used to decorate church interiors. Pearls and precious stones were widely used in old Russian embroidery techniques. A remarkable piece of fine embroidery work is the draperie "The Virgin of Vladimir" from the robing room of the Cathedral of the Assumption. Crafted at the Tsarina's sewing shop at the Kremlin, it looks more like an icon clad in a golden frame and ornamented with pearls and precious stones.

One of the most interesting parts of the exhibition is hosted by the **Church of the Twelve Apostles**, a domestic church of the Russian patriarchs. Over centuries, its interior was altered several times: the windows were widened and

The iconostasis of the Church of the Twelve Apostles.

the iconostasis renovated. Modern-day restoration experts were able to replicate the late 17th century interior of the church. The old iconostasis did not survive. The existing one was transferred to the church from the Ascen- sion convent of the Moscow Kremlin in 1929. The magnificent five-tier iconostasis of carved gilded wood was crafted in the customary 17th century Moscow baroque style noted for its richness of ornamental motifs and ex-

Icon of the Veneration of the Cross. Moscow. 1677-1678 (?).

pressiveness. The sumptuous ornamentation is interlarded with pictorial representations of flowers, fruits and creeping grape vines.

The church houses a display of 17th century icons most of which belonged to the Kremlin cathedrals and monasteries.

The chronological arrangement of the exhibits makes it possible to trace the evolution of the Russian art of icon painting in the 17th century, the so-called "Stroganoff" school, and to get a better idea of the works by the tsar's icon painters of the second half of the 17th century.

The Stroganoff school icons "elevated the soul" and "gladdened the eye"; they were painted to please the aesthetic tastes of persons with keen discrimination in matters of art. The term "Stroganoff school" was associated with the patronage of arts by the "eminent Stroganoff family" who had their own icon painting shops in the town of Solvychegodsk in the Urals. The period from 1660 to the end of the 17th century witnessed the departure from the traditional old Russian icon painting style. Signs of a new trend in pictorial art, later termed as "realistic", could be discerned in the icons "Theodore Stratilatus", "St. Andrew", "The Crucifixion" and other works by Simon Ushakov, Fyodor Zubov and Fyodor Rozhnov. These works reveal the artists' mindfulness of the surrounding world, the natural scenery and the human environment.

The exhibits displayed at the Museum of Applied Art and Life Style of 17th century Russia provide an overview of the aesthetic tastes and preferences of the Russian society in the 17th century and give a clue to the understanding of the spiritual life of people during the transition from medieval to modern history.

The Patriarch's Palace and the Church of the Twelve Apostles are among the most spectacular architectural sights of the Moscow Kremlin. Their splendid interiors and the articles displayed at the Kremlin museums testify to the outstanding talents of the artists and crafsmen who created the timeless masterpieces of the Russian culture.

Cathedral Square is closed from the eastern side by the magnificient architectural ensemble – the *Belfry of Ivan the Great*, with the *Assumption Bell Tower* and the *Filaret Tower*.

The belfry was built by Italian architect Bono Friazin in 1505 – 1508 and consisted of two lower, and part of a third, tiers and was 60 metres high. At that time it dominated the architectural ensemble of Cathedral Square. The belfry got its name after St. John the Climacus to whom the church built in 1392 in the first tier was consecrated. In 1600, by order of Tsar Boris Godunov the belfry was brought up to the height of 81 metres. The tier structure of the belfry only emphasizes its height. An inscription in golden letters under the golden dome has the names of Tsar Boris Godunov, his son Fyodor and the date of its raising.

Several staircases lead to the upper tiers of the Belfry of Ivan the Great. At first there is an inner stone staircase of 83 steps, then a spiral staircase of 149 steps and lastly, a spiral metal staircase of 97 steps.

The belfry served as a watch and signal tower of the Kremlin. One could see an expanse of some 25 to 30 kilometres from top, and a beautiful view of Moscow opened from it.

In 1532 – 1543 architect Petroch the Younger built a church with a bell tower to the north face of the belfry, and in 1624 stone mason Bazhen Ogurtsov, on order of Patriarch Filaret, the father of Mikhail Romanov, added another structure to the church – the so-called Filaret Tower. It was intended for putting on the main bell of the Romanov dynasty.

All these buildings formed a picturesque and integral architectural com-

The Belfry of Ivan the Great, the Assumption Bell Tower and the Filaret Tower.

position, despite the fact that they had been erected at different times.

Muscovites compared the belfry with a burning candle, or with a warrior in a golden helmet. It is by right considered one of the most beautiful struc-

tures of the Russian architecture of the 16th century.

Both towers were blown up by Napoleon's troops during their hasty retreat from Moscow in 1812. The Belfry of Ivan the Great was not destroyed, but

The Tsar Bell.

only cracked. It was due to the craftsmanship and skill of its buiders and its exceptionally solid structure and size, so unusual for its time. In 1819 the Bell Tower and the Filaret Tower were restored by architect D.I. Gilardi.

At present the first floor of the Bell Tower houses an exhibition hall of the Moscow Kremlin State Historical and Cultural Museum-Monument.

There are 21 bells on the belfry and the Bell Tower made in the 16th – 19th centuries. They are outstanding specimens of monumental castings associated with the names of Russian craftsmen Fyodor and Ivan Motorin, Vasili

V.S. Sadovnikov. Festive gathering in Ivanovskaya Square, with the turn-out of the royal family. Water color. 1851.

and Yakov Leontyev, Andrei Chokhov, Filipp Andreyev.

Some of the bells were given names – "Novy", "Reut" and "Uspensky". The latter is the largest, it weighs about 70 tons and was cast by master Zavyalov in 1517 – 1519.

The traditional Russian art of bell-ringing is revived in our day. Complex work has been done to restore and modernize the bells on the Assumption Bell Tower.

On Russian Orthodox Christmas, January 7, 1994, bell-ringing in the Kremlin was resumed, after a 76-year interval.

Moscow has now heard the voice of the Kremlin bells again.

Near the Belfry of Ivan the Great there is the famous **Tsar Bell**, a unique work of master-craftsmen of the 18th century. It was cast in 1733 – 1735 in the Kremlin by Ivan Motorin and his son Mikhail.

The Tsar Cannon.

Russian master-craftsmen V. Kobelev, N. Galkin, N. Kokhtev and N. Serebryakov adorned the bell with relief ornament and pictures of Empress Anna Ivanovna and Tsar Alexei Mikhailovich. There are inscriptions in decorative cartouches with baroque volutes and angels on the rims, telling the bell's history. The Tsar Bell is the world's biggest. Its weight is over 200 tons, height – 6.14 metres and diameter – 6.6 metres.

During the fire in 1737 the bell was in the foundry pit. The red-hot metal cracked because of uneven cooling when the fire was being extinguished. A piece weighing 11.5 tons broke off the bell. The bell remained in the pit for 100 years after that. In 1836 architect A.A. Montferrand worked out a plan to raise it and place on a special pedestal.

The square behind the Belfry of Ivan the Great was named *Ivanovskaya*. This is where the buildings of *prikazes* (department) stood. Tsar's decrees were announced there. Prikaz officials shouted very loudly so that they could be heard in all corners of the square. Since then there has been a saying in

The Arsenal building.

Russia: *To scream at the top of one's voice so that all Ivanovskaya Square could hear.*

There is another interesting sight in the square – the **Tsar Cannon**, which is another example of monumental artistic casting of the 16th century. It was cast of bronze by Andrei Chokhov in 1586, during the reign of Tsar Fyodor Ivanovich, son of Ivan the Terrible. The weight of the the Tsar Cannon is 40 tons, its caliber – 890 millimetres and length – 5.34 metres. It is the world's biggest cannon in caliber, which was why it got its name. It was meant to be used for defending the Moscow Kremlin and was positioned at the Spassky Gate.

The barrel of the cannon is decorated with ornament and relief inscriptions telling its history. There is also a cast image of Tsar Fyodor Ivanovich sitting on horse and holding a sceptre in his hand.

An iron decorative gun-carriage designed for the Tsar Cannon by architect A.P. Bryullov was cast at the Berd's plant in St.Petersburg in 1835. The cannon balls beside it are purely decorative and weigh one ton each.

Old cannons placed along the Arsenal wall.

There is the **Arsenal** building between the Troitskaya and Nikolskaya towers in the western part of the Kremlin. Its construction began in 1702.

The general design of the building belonged to Peter the Great. The construction was supervised by architects D. Ivanov and G. Konrad. However, in 1706 the work on it was interrupted due to the war with Sweden. Construction was resumed in 1722 and completed in 1736.

A year later the Arsenal was destroyed in a big fire. Its restoration took place during the 1786–1796 period and was directed and supervised by engineer L.Gerard and architect M. Kazakov. In 1812 the building suffered again from an explosion during the retreat of Napoleon's army from Moscow. The restoration work was completed by archi-

tects A. Bakarev, I. Mironovsky, I. Tamansky and E. Tyurin in 1828.

The Arsenal building, trapeziform in plan view, with a large inner yard and two entrance arches, was built of brick and faced with white stone. The height of its walls is 24 metres. Originally, arms and ammunition were stored in the Arsenal. The most valuable military trophies were supposed to be kept there. Later, it was decided to open a Museum of the Patriotic War of 1812 in the Arsenal. More than 800 cannons were placed along its south-eastern wall, most of which had been captured by the Russian Army and guerilla units from Napoleon's troops during their retreat in 1812. The bronze barrels of the cannons were cast in Paris, Lyons, Breslau and other European cities in 1790 – 1810. Especially valuable are

The Senate building.

20 Russian cannons of the 16th – 17th century made by Russian gunsmiths, among them A. Chokhov ("Troil" cannon, 1590), M. Osipov ("Gamayun" cannon, 1690) and Y. Dubina ("Wolf" cannon, 1659).

On the southern wall of the Arsenal, at the entrance arch, a plaque was mounted in memory of the soldiers shot during the revolutionary events in October 1917. Another plaque was mounted in 1965 in commemoration of the men and officers of the Kremlin garrison who died defending Moscow and the Moscow Kremlin from Nazi air raids during the Great Patriotic War of 1941 – 1945.

The **Senate** building is rightly considered a fine example of Russian architecture of the 18th century in the complex of the Moscow Kremlin. This structure was designed by the outstanding Russian architect M.F. Kazakov. Construction work lasted from 1776 until 1788, and the interior decoration was completed in 1790. Originally, it was intended for the assemblies of the Moscow Gubernia nobility. In 1856, in connection with the transfer of two Senate departments from St.Petersburg to Moscow, it was given over to the judicial departments – the Moscow Senate.

This three-storey building has, in plan view, the shape of a blunt-ended triangle. There is a large green dome over one of the angles of the triangle. The building stands opposite the Senatskaya Tower, which is confronted on the outer side of the Kremlin wall by the Mausoleum in Red Square. This great dome on the building was initially crowned with the crest of Moscow – an equestrian statue of St.George.

In 1856, when the building was taken up by judicial departments, the crest was replaced by the emblem of royal justice – a pillar on books and a crown with an inscription *"Law"*. And in 1918, when Russia's capital was transferred from Petrograd to Moscow, a red flag was hoisted on the dome, now replaced by a three-colour flag of the Russian Federation.

The Senate building is a brilliant example of early Russian classicism in architecture. Severe and well-balanced outwardly, it revealed the rich opportunities of a new style in beautiful and varied decor.

A big circular hall, which is a real masterpiece of Russian architecture, is most impressive. It was called at various times *Bely, Yekaterininsky and Sverdlovsky*. The hall is surrounded by perimeter with light columns and pilasters of the Corinthian order. There is a narrow gallery with two tiers of plaster bas-relief replicas of portraits of Russian tsars and princes between the windows. Their marble originals were created by the famous Russian sculptor F.I. Shubin in 1774 – 1775 for the Chesmensky Palace in St.Petersburg. One can now see them in the Armoury.

The hall has a huge spherical cupola, 24.7 metres in diameter and 27-metre-high. Over the door arches there are high-reliefs with allegoric scenes glorifying Empress Catherine the Great (sculptor G.T. Zamarayev). The hall was called "Yekaterininsky" in her honour.

The white and blue walls, snow-white columns, the blue upholstery of the furniture, the golden rosettes of the cupola, the light, clear-cut lines and immaculate proportions of all details make the interior of the hall perfect, both artistically and architecturally.

Situated inside a magnificent rotunda, this hall is not detected from the outside. Only a gigantic cupola, which can be seen from a distance, marks the location of the compositional centre of the entire building.

The *Oval Hall* is under the second, smaller cupola. It is also white and blue in colour, like the Yekaterininsky Hall. Right under the cupola are high-reliefs of St.George.

The flat and study of V.I. Lenin, the head of the Soviet government, were in the Senate building from 1918 until 1924. The government of the country worked here until recently. After reconstruction there is now the residence of the President of the Russian Federation.

Opposite the Arsenal building, the Kremlin Palace of Congresses was constructed in 1960 – 1961, now the **State Kremlin Palace**. It is connected with the Great Kremlin Palace by two passages with a small winter garden. The pylons of the building are faced with white marble. The glass walls of the palace reflect the buildings surrounding the palace, as if trying to conceal its alien look, compared with the harmonious architectural ensemble of the ancient Kremlin.

The palace was intended for party congresses, sessions of the USSR Supreme Soviet and various conferences and meetings. It could also be used for theatre performances, concerts, receptions, festivals, etc.

The State Kremlin Palace is the biggest public building in Moscow: it has 800 rooms of various size. The central hall of the palace was Europe's larg-

The Tomb of the Unknown Soldier.

est. It seats about 6,000 people on an area of 5.6 thousand square metres. Important state functions and international congresses are held here.

Landscape gardening was a matter of attention and pride in Rus from olden times. As is known, back in the 15th century the *Tsar's Garden* was laid out opposite the Kremlin on the bank of the Moskva River. During the reign of Ivan the Terrible there was the *Aptekarsky* (Medicinal) *Garden* on the right bank of the Neglinka River, between the Troitsky (Trinity) and Borovitsky gates.

The art of landscape gardening in the Kremlin especially flourished in the 17th century. The list of the Kremlin gardens of the time included the "upper", "palace", "room" and "embankment" gardens. The latter – *Upper* and *Lower* gardens – commanded special attention.

The Upper Garden was on the roof of the two-storey palace of Boris Godunov. The Lower Garden was laid out on the roof of a building "*next to the Embankment Chamber at the Tainitsky Gate*".

The *Kremlin Garden* renamed ***Alexandrovsky*** in 1856 is a good specimen of landscape gardening of the first quarter of the 19th century. It was laid out in 1822 – 1823 along the Kremlin wall, above the old bed of the Neglinka River. It was connected with the general reconstruction of Moscow after the fire in 1812 and supervised by architect O.I. Bovet.

The iron gate of the main entrance and the fence with decorative bronze elements were made after E. Pascal's sketches. The side fence along Manezhnaya Street was erected in 1934.

Near the Middle Arsenalnaya Tower there is a grotto, a typical feature of the 19th-century landscape gardening. It was designed by O.I. Bovet and made on an artificial mound. The grotto was adorned with fragments of white-stone ornaments from buildings pulled down after 1812. On its outer platform an orchestra played during public festivities.

In 1913, close to the main gate of the garden, an obelisk was erected in honour of the tercentenary of the Romanov dynasty. In 1918, on order of new power, the names of "*outstanding world revolutionaries*" were hewn on its sides.

In 1870, the *Tainitsky Garden* was planted on the southern slope of Borovitsky Hill.

In 1940, the *Big Kremlin Public Garden* was laid out on the site of the former Dragoon drill ground in the southern part of Ivanovskaya Square.

Yuri Gagarin, the world's first cosmonaut, has planted an oak named "Cosmos" to commemorate the first ever space flight of man.

In 1967, the **Tomb of the Unknown Soldier** was erected at the Kremlin wall in the Alexandrovsky Garden. The remains of an unknown defender of Moscow from a common grave at the village of Kryukovo were brought and reburied here.

The *Eternal Flame* is burning in memory of those killed during the Great Patriotic War (1941-1945).

THE ARMOURY

The world-famous *Armoury (Oruzhei-naya palata* in Russian) is one of the oldest museums of Russia, a virtual treasure-house. It got its name from one of the Kremlin workshops. The Russian word "palata" has several meanings: palace, stone house, mansion, chambers. The name given to this museum is absolutely original and has no analogues in Russia.

The collection of treasures for the Kremlin museum began way back in the late 14th – early 15th century, at the time of the formation of the Russian centralized state, when items of great historical and artistic value began to be stored in the Grand Prince's treasury. At first the treasury was housed in a special chamber of the Cathedral of the Annunciation. On order of Grand Prince Ivan III a special building – the Treasury Court – was erected between the Archangel Cathedral and the Cathedral of the Annunciation in 1485. A greater part of its collection consisted of items made by the Moscow Kremlin workshops.

The Armoury as a depository of tsar's treasures was first mentioned in chronicles at the beginning of the 16th century. The changes in the fate of the tsar's treasure-house were connected with the name of Peter the Great. By his decree issued in 1718, tsar's garments and precious regalia had to be exhibited in oak cases behind glass walls. That was the prototype of the future museum.

In 1806 – 1812, at the Troitsky Gates a special building for the Armoury was erected designed by architect I.V. Yegotov, in place of the former palace of Boris Godunov. Work on interior decoration was started, but the grim and turbulent year 1812 began, and the Kremlin treasures were evacuated to Nizhni Novgorod. In 1814 they were returned to Moscow and placed in seven halls of the buildings where they remained until the middle of the 19th century. However, the premises were unfit for keeping the treasures which could perish from cold and dampness. A special two-storey building was constructed by famous architect K.A.Ton for the Armoury in 1851, which became part of the ensemble of the Great Kremlin Palace. It was situated in the south-western section of the Kremlin, where the former Equestrian prikaz had

*N.A. Burdin. A hall of the Armoury
disigned by architect I. Yegotov.*

stood. The facade of the building overlooking the Moskva River was faced by carved white-stoned decorations, in resemblance of the architectural style of the 17th century.

There are nine halls in the museum – four on the ground floor and five on the first floor, with a total area of 2,500 square metres. More than four thousand items are exhibited in fifty-five showcases in the halls.

The world's richest collection of ***Russian gold and silverware of the 12th –***

early 20th centuries is placed in the first two halls on the first floor. Looking at these works by Russian gold- and silversmiths one cannot fail to notice their exquisite, graceful pattern and the virtuoso technique of their execution. The items on display make it possible to trace the eight-century evolution of jeweller's technique and artistic styles, and the formation of national original features. There are exhibits which show the flourishing of artistic handicrafts in Rus before the Tatar-Mongol

The Armoury.

invasion, items made by Moscow silversmiths in the 15th – 17th centuries, masters of Novgorod, Pskov, Solvychegodsk, towns in the Volga area, Moscow and St.Petersburg in the 18th – 19th centuries, as well as by a number of jeweller firms of the latter half of the 19th – early 20th centuries.

Visitors to the museum have a chance to get acquainted with the early history of goldsmiths' work – archaeological artifacts and items of Byzantine, Southern Slavonic and Georgian art works, which open the exposition.

Early Russian art was greatly influenced by Byzantium, which had close ties with the traditions of ancient art. The specific features of ancient art can be seen in the earliest item of the Armoury collection – a silver jug made circa 400 A.D. in Constantinople *(showcase 1)*. Nine muses depicted on it were a favourite motif of ancient master-craftsmen.

Cloisonne enamels are considered to be a remarkable achievement of Byzantine masters of the 10th – 12th centuries, a period of the greatest flourishing of Byzantine art.

A small 11th –century icon "Crucifixion" is a fine example of this technique *(showcase 1)*.

Items of Russian jewellers' art, 17th – 20th century.
(Hall 2).

The Armoury boasts one of the world's best collections of Byzantine *cameos* (gems carved in relief). Particularly wonderful is a 12th-century chrysoprase cameo, "The Assumption of the Virgin", which used to be part of Patriarch Joseph's II *panagia*-icon *(showcase 1)*.

Necklet and pendant.
Ryazan, 12th century.

Treasure troves give us an idea about jewellery art of pre-Mongolian Rus. The Armoury collection contains finely executed articles made by goldsmiths of that time. Among them are women's decorations: head-dress pendants, necklets, rings and bracelets. Items from the famous Ryazan trove, such as gold necklets and head-dress pendants, refer to the 12th – early 13th century *(showcase 2)*. Their masterly execution is truly amazing. The images of saints were made in cloisonne encircled by a multi-tier interlace filigree pattern.

A 12th-century chalice for the Eucharist made by masters in Vladimir-Suzdal Rus *(showcase 2)* is a magnificent example of silverwork. The chalice is connected with the name of Prince Yuri Dolgoruky, the legendary founder of Moscow.

The last quarter of the 15th century – the rule of Ivan III – was a significant period in the development of Moscow jewellery art. The best craftsmen created priceless church plate for the newly-built cathedrals in the Moscow Kremlin. Among the exibits are the censer dating to 1489 *(showcase 3)* from the Cathedral of the Annunciation, and two silver reliquaries dating to 1486 – the "Great Zion" and "Small Zion" *(showcase 4)* shaped as single-domed churches from the Cathedral of the Assumption.

Chalice for the Eucharist. Moscow, 1598. Tsarina Irina Godunova's present to the Archangel Cathedral in the Moscow Kremlin.

In the beginning of the 16th century "golden-domed" Moscow became the gatherer and unifier of Russian lands. Skilled craftsmen from all over Rus created precious articles in the Moscow Kremlin workshops, which decorated palaces and were used at court ceremonies and church services.

Foreign master-craftsmen also worked in the Kremlin side by side with their

Small Zion.
1913 replica of the lost original. Moscow. 1486.

Russian counterparts. The art of Russian masters, enriched by foreign artistic culture, retained its original national character.

Moscow jewellers in the 16th century reached a high level of perfection in applying various techniques to working with precious metals and stones, especially the technique of engraving

Censer.
Moscow Kremlin workshops. 1616.

and niello. A gold dish made in 1561 and weighing three kilos *(showcase 5)* by order of Tsar Ivan the Terrible for the Kabardian Princess Maria Temryukovna is distinguished by exquis-ite simplicity and classical perfection. The gold shrine of 1589 which belonged to Tsarina Irina, the wife of Tsar Fyodor Ivanovich, and the censer of 1589 from the Archangel Cathedral

Gospel.
Moscow. Master G. Ovdokimov. 1632.

(*showcase 5*) are real masterpieces. Among jewellery items dating to the time of Ivan the Terrible there are wonderful gold filigree enamelled icon frameworks and the gold cover of the 1571 Gospel from the Cathedral of the Annunciation (*showcase 6*). The cover was picked out in delicate filigree with big semiprecious stones set into it in high chased casts.

Dipper of Tsar Mikhail Fyodorovich Romanov.
Moscow Kremlin workshops. 1618.

Traditions and innovations were combined in the 17th-century art, and the foundations of the secular culture for subsequent centuries were laid. Jewellery work of that time is distinguished by sumptuous decorations and the use of multicoloured enamels and precious stones.

A tendency to polychromy can be traced in the works by the outstanding Moscow silversmith Gavrila Ovdokimov. An example is furnished by the cover of the 1632 Gospel *(showcase 6)* presented by Tsar Mikhail Fyodorovich Romanov to the Trinity-St.Sergius Monastery.

The covers of the shrines of Tsarevich Dmitri (from the Archangel Cathedral) and St.Cyril of Belozersk, a prominent enlightener of the Russian Middle Ages, donated by Boyar F.I. Sheremetev to the Monastery of St. Cyril of Belozersk, are unique samples of Russian plastic art of the 17th century *(showcase 8)*.

A chalice of 1635 *(showcase 14)* presented by Patriarch Nikon to Tsar Alexei Mikhailovich is a real masterpiece of enamel work.

Gold and silver tableware was regarded a necessary attribute of the 17th-century court life. Traditionally made at the Kremlin workshops, it imitated wooden and ceramic tableware. Richly decorated *bratinas* (loving-cups) used to be passed around by those sitting at the table *(showcase 10)*. They usually bear the names of their owners or didactic texts inscribed in intricate ligature on the edge of the cups.

Discos and zvezditsa – attributes of religious ceremony.
Moscow. 1664.

Gold and silver dippers were used for drinking red and white mead *(showcase 10)*. Their exquisite shapes and fine niello (sulphureous alloy of copper, lead and silver) pattern rims with pearls and uncut gem-stones make these creations of master-jewellers especially attractive.

The gold dippers which belonged to Tsar Mikhail Fyodorovich and were used at gala receptions in the Facets Palace, as well as small cups for drinking hard liquor, goblets, bowls, glasses and plates for serving meat, fowl and other food, are truly gorgeous *(showcase 10)*.

Gold and silverwork of the 18th – early 19th century occupies a special place in the Armoury collection. A secular trend emerged in Russian art at the time of radical economic and political transformations carried out by Peter the Great.

In 1712 St.Petersburg became the capital of Russia. Quite a few masters and artists from West European countries were invited to build and decorate the new capital. Gold- and silversmiths were brought there from Moscow.

A new style, "Petrin baroque", came into being in Russian art. Jewellery items were now decorated with em-

*Breastplate with a portrait
of Peter the Great.
Russia. Early 18th century.*

bossed, high-relief elements in the form of scallop-shells, scrolls and cartouches. Acanthus leaves and tulip flowers prevailed in floral ornaments. At that time enamelled portrait miniatures of Peter the Great appeared which, as a rule, decorated snuffboxes *(showcase 15).*

In the 1740s – 1760s articles made of precious metals in rococo style were decorated with cast and embossed high-relief designs. The use of many articles and their form and decorations had changed by that time. Award dippers with massive cast eagles resemble beautiful vases *(showcase 16)*. Tea and coffee services, samovars, milk jugs, sugar-bowls and teapots on supports began to appear in Russia. Church plate was decorated in a similar style.

In the third quarter of the 18th century rococo style was gradually replaced by classicism. The flat surface of articles was now decorated with elements borrowed from ancient art – vases, garlands, olive and oak branches, and scallop-shells engraved and embossed in low relief. Blue-grey enamel was often used.

Goblets, dishes, services of china and church plate were distinguished by

Gospel. Print – Moscow, 1698; cover – St.Petersburg.
Master H. Unger. 1794.

extreme finery, masterly execution and balance of proportion and colours. A gold snuffbox of 1784 *(showcase 18)* made to order of Count P.B. Sheremetev by jeweller G. Ador is a magnificient example of Russian classicism. At the time jewellers mainly used diamonds for decorating their items. The Gospel of 1794 made by talented Petersburg master H. Unger *(showcase 18)* is decorated with a lattice of 2,500 cut diamonds, aquamarines and amethysts. It was donated by Empress Catherine the Great to the Alexander Nevsky Monastery.

Big jewellery firms were set up in Moscow and St.Petersburg at the time, such as Sazikov (1793), Faberge (1842),

*Easter egg with model of Alexandrovsky Palace.
St.Petersburg. Master H. Wigstrom. 1908.*

Ovchinnikov (1853), Grachev (1856) and Khlebnikov (1860). Items made by them are exhibited in *showcases 20 and 21*.

The articles of the famous firm of Carl Faberge merit special attention. The Armoury collection has the best items created by the firm – precious Easter eggs with surprises inside *(showcase 20)*, which were annually ordered by members of the royal family from 1885 onwards. Each of these unique articles took almost a year to produce. The first such Easter eggs were made by talented jeweller M.E. Perkhin. In 1891 he made a gold and platinum model of the battle cruiser "Pamyat Azova" (Memory of Azov) on an aquamarine support, which was enclosed in a heliotrope egg. The egg's surface was decorated with applied gold ornament in rococo style and diamonds.

The same master made an exquisite gold egg-shaped clock decorated with a bunch of onyx lilies. One of the unsurpassed masterpieces of Faberge was a mechanical gold model of a Trans-Siberian express train with a platinum locomotive, placed inside a silver egg with the inscription on the surface: "The Great Trans-Siberian Railway by 1900".

Chain mail.
Moscow. Late 16th century.

Helmet. Moscow Kremlin workshops.
Master N. Davydov. 1621.

A miniature model of the Alexandrovsky Palace in Tsarskoye Selo (near St.Petersburg) is enclosed in a nephrite egg. It was made by Petersburg jeweller Heinrich Wigstrom and presented by Tsar Nicholas II to Empress Alexandra Fyodorovna for Easter in 1908.

A stylized model of the Moscow Kremlin was made as a music box. There is an egg in the centre crowned with the golden dome of the Cathedral of the Assumption. The interior of the cathedral can be seen through the windows on the egg's surface, and there are massive Kremlin walls with four towers along its perimeter.

These works evoke great admiration by their fine execution, original artistic solutions and a great variety of the materials used.

The next two halls of the Armoury – No 3 and No 4 – contain **arms and armour made in the 12th – 19th centuries**. There are various samples of Russian, West European and Oriental combat arms and ceremonial and hunting weapons, as well as armour and chain-mails to protect the rider and his horse. Each of these exhibits is of a high artistic and historical value. All of them are connected with the formation and development of the Russian state and the royal court's life. The shape, pattern and decorations of the Russian armour are quite original *(hall 4)*. The main part of a Russian warrior's armour was the chain-mail, a kind of tunic made of small interlocked metal rings. There were several varieties of chain-mail armour differing in their make: *baidana*, *bakhterets* and

THE MOSCOW KREMLIN

Full suit of ceremonial armour for rider and horse.
Germany. Master K. Lochner. 16th century.

yushman (showcase 27). The forged damascene-steel helmet of Tsar Mikhail Fyodorovich Romanov is a sort of a symbol of the Russian warriors. This wonderful sample of fine jewellery work was made by talented Russian master-craftsman Nikita Davydov. The Kremlin workshops produced remarkable hunting firearms *(showcase 27)*. Ceremonial arms of the 18th – 19th centuries made by master-craftsmen of the leading centres of Russian arms production – Tula, Olonets, Sestroretsk, St.Petersburg and Zlatoust – take a worthy place in the Armoury collection *(showcase 29)*.

There are relics on display, which reflect spectacular events of Russian history, for instance, the sabres which belonged to Kuzma Minin and Dmitry Pozharsky *(showcase 27)*, and military trophies captured by the Russian army under the command of Peter the Great, which defeated the Swedes at Poltava in 1709. These include Swedish pistols, swords, drums, kettle-drums and banner heads *(showcase 29)*. There is also a sabre forged by Ivan Bushuyev from Zlatoust. Its damascene-steel blade is decorated with scenes depicting the liberation of the Bulgarian fortress of Varna by the Russian army during the 1828 – 1829 Russo-Turkish war. In *showcases 22 – 24* of the hall No 3 there are works by armourers from Holland, Germany, England, Italy and France. These are samples of tournament armour, side-arms and firearms. The centerpiece of the exposition is a full suit of ceremonial armour protecting both the rider and his horse. It was made by the famous German master Kunz Lochner and presented by Polish King Stefan Batory to Tsar Fyodor Ivanovich in 1584 *(showcase 23)*. *Showcases 25* and *26* demonstrate works by armourers from Iran and Turkey of the 16th – 17th centuries. Their rich decoration conformed to the aesthetic tastes of the Russian nobility of the time.

The unique ceremonial shield of Prince F.M. Mstislavsky made in Iran in the 16th century is truly priceless. Its surface is embossed with spiral strips and inlaid with ornamental and figure compositions *(showcase 26)*.

The big collection of **West European silverware of the 13th – 19th centuries** *(hall 5)* is truly world-famous. It includes gifts from other countries to the royal family presented by foreign ambassadors and articles brought to Russia by merchants.

The unique collection of the Armoury illustrates the history of Russia's political and trade ties with other countries. It also acquaints visitors with artistic trends in jewellery work and shows the mastery of jewellers in England, Germany, Holland, Denmark, Poland, Sweden and France.

The English exhibits in the collection are truly amazing *(showcase 31)*.

There are royal gifts to Russian tsars and acquisitions made by trade agents during the period from the mid-16th to the mid-17th century.

The earliest exhibit is the pickle bowl of 1557 – 1558 *(showcase 31)* presented to Ivan the Terrible by Anthony Jenkinson, one of the first English ambassadors to Moscow. The form and character of the decorations of this bowl used for serving all sorts of pickled delicacies and sweetmeats show

that it is obviously a work of the late Renaissance.

The massive silver wine flagons in the shape of heraldic leopards of 1600 – 1601 *(showcase 31)* are among the best items of the collection.

The collection of Swedish ambassadorial gifts is the biggest in the exposition of artistic silverware presented by foreign ambassadors. It includes articles made by famous master-craftsmen from Nuremberg, Augsburg and Hamburg, whose works were highly valued in Western Europe. A considerable part of them was brought to Moscow by envoys of Queen Christina, King Charles X, King Charles XI and King Charles XII from 1647 to 1699. They include luxurious huge goblets, dishes, multi-tier pickle bowls, vases for fruit and globe-shaped vessels. One of them – "Celestial Globe" – is a table wine fountain *(showcase 33)*.

The collection of gold- and silverware of the late 16th – early 18th centuries by masters of Hamburg is especially numerous (about 300 items in all). Among them are works by the well-known master Jacob Mores the Elder: wonderful, richly decorated silver goblets and a wine horn.

The unusual shape of fumigators is simply astonishing. One of them was made by outstanding master-craftsman Dietrich Utermarke *(showcase 39)*. These fumigators adorned a cupboard of Tsar Mikhail Fyodorovich Romanov in the 17th century.

The collection of Nuremberg silverware numbers 265 items made by 120 masters. There are original pumpkin-, apple-, pear-, and pineapple-shaped goblets, double and triple goblets, figure-goblets, fountain-goblets and ship-goblets. The Armoury has a wonder-

Wine flagon in the form of heraldic leopard. London. 1600 – 1601.

ful vessel of 1595 in the shape of an eagle with extended wings *(showcase 35)*, made by the head of the Nuremberg school of goldsmiths, C. Jamnitzer, in the latter half of the 16th century.

The Augsburg silverwork of the latter half of the 17th – the first half of the 18th century in the museum collection is distinguished by sumptuous and varied decorations. The goblet with a figure of Diana, the Goddess of hunting,

Fumigator. Germany, Hamburg.
Master D. Utermarkt, c.1600.

on a raindeer, and bowls in the shape of a lion and a mounted warrior merit special attention. Augsburg masters also made decorative basins with pictures from the Bible, and ancient myths and history *(showcases 33, 40)*.

A collection of French silverwork of the 17th century is small, but very valuable. In 1649 a dish and a wash jug *(showcase 41)* were made in Paris and presented by King Charles II of England to Tsar Alexei Mikhailovich.

The beautiful "Orlov" silver tea service was made in France in 1770 on order of Empress Catherine the Great as a gift to Count G. Orlov. The "Orlov" service has more than 3,000 pieces *(showcase 41)*.

Hall 5.
West European silverware. 13th – 19th century.

The china service known as "Olympic" *(showcase 43)* was a diplomatic gift from Napoleon I to Emperor Alexander I on the occasion of the signing of the Tilsit peace treaty in 1807.

A collection of ***valuable fabrics, old Russian secular and church dress and gala costumes of the16th – early 20th centuries*** is on display in the ground floor halls of the museum.

Hall 6.
Precious fabrics, obverse and ornamental embroidery, 14th – 18th century;
secular dress of 16th – early 20th century.

The Armoury is justly proud of samples of artistic needlework of the 16th – 18th centuries *(showcase 46)*.

Palls, shrouds and shrouds of Christ are the most interesting and beautiful samples of ancient Russian artistic culture. Coloured silk, golden thread and pearls were used to embroider not only images, but whole intricate compositions. Early Russian embroidery could be called "fine needle painting".

Pearl embroidery with geometrical or foliate patterns decorate the collars, hems and cuffs of sakkos and chasubles and sacerdotal robes of the highest clergy. Russian embroideresses masterfully combined small and large pearls with gold plates and gem-stones against a background covered with small spangles.

The work of the embroideresses of the Tsarina's workshop in the Kremlin is distinguished by rare mastery and technique.

Valuable Iranian and Turkish fabrics such as silk and velvet were widely used in the 16th – 17th centuries for making ceremonial attire of the tsars and the highest clergy *(shawcases 44, 46)* and decorating thrones, carriages and saddles.

Later, Italian fabrics, along with Oriental ones, were also brought to Russia. The famous Italian silk velvet was

THE MOSCOW KREMLIN

Mitre.
Moscow Kremlin workshops. 1634.

used to make home *kaftans* of Patriarch Nikon, whose wardrobe was not inferior to that of the tsar himself.

The ceremonial kaftans of Peter the Great and the sakkos of Patriarch Nikon *(showcase 46)* were made of samite.

Kaftan was the most popular ancient Russian garment worn by both men and women.

Warm kaftans were fur-lined and had long sleeves for wear outdoors. Fitted kaftans were worn every day and on ceremonial occasions with proper decorations.

The Armoury collection boasts the rich wardrobes of the tsars Alexei Mikhai-lovich and Peter the Great *(showcase 44)*.

A characteristic feature of old Russian clothes was the wide use of pearls in trimming and decoration.

Pearls were used for head-dresses, earrings, rings and pendants. Even ceremonial footwear was embroidered with pearls.

There is a wide variety of accessories of old Russian clothes in the Armoury collection.

One of the showcases displays head-dresses. There is one which was worn by Tsarina Anastasia, the wife of Ivan the Terrible, who died in 1560. It was taken from her tomb and restored by

Catherine the Great's coronation dress.
Russia. 1762.

specialists of the Kremlin museum *(showcase 44)*.

Luxurious royal garments astonished foreign guests who thought that *"a small part of this wealth would have been sufficient to decorate a dozen of countries"*.

Ceremonial dresses, kaftans and jackets of the 18ᵗʰ – 19ᵗʰ centuries *(showcase 45)* were made in accordance with European fashion.

The earliest sample of woman's dress in the collection is the coronation robe of Empress Catherine the Great, and the latest – the coronation robe of 1896.

A collection of **precious regalia and articles of royal court ceremonies of the 13ᵗʰ – 19ᵗʰ centuries** *(hall 7)* is Russia's national pride. Family relics passed from father to son represent a kind of a chronicle of the Russian state, they were witness of the most important events of its history.

The *Cap of Monomachus* of the late 13ᵗʰ – early 14ᵗʰ century made by an unknown master-craftsman *(showcase 50)* is one of the most well-known exhibits in the precious collection.

There is a host of legends about its origin and name. According to one of them, it was presented to the Grand

Cap of Monomachus.
Late 13th – early 14th century.

Prince of Kiev Vladimir Monomachus, by the Byzantine Emperor Konstantin Monomachus, and was named after him. This legend was supported in every way possible in Russia, for it goes to prove that the Russian princes and tsars succeeded to the Byzantine emperors.

According to Nikon's chronicle of the 17th century, Dmitry, a grandson of Prince Ivan III, was crowned with the Cap of Monomachus when he was elected to be the Grand Prince. Evidently, the ceremony was meant to emphasize the might of Moscow power and the growing strength of the Rus-

sian state. From the late 15th to the late 17th century all Russian monarchs, except Peter the Great, were crowned with the Cap of Monomachus.

There were other crowns used on ceremonial occasions.

The ceremonial precious crown of Tsar Ivan the Terrible known as the *Kazan Cap* of the 16th century *(showcase 50)* is magnificent.

The *Grand Set* – a crown, an orb and a sceptre made for Tsar Mikhail Fyodorovich Romanov in the 17th century is regarded a beautiful sample of artistic craftsmanship and high taste. There is the *Cap of Monomachus of the second*

Crown of Empress Anna Ivanovna.
St.Petersburg. 1730.

order in the collection. Its origin and use were connected with the coronation of 10-year-old Peter (future Emperor Peter the Great) and his elder brother Ivan in 1682. The dual reign of the two minor tsars Ivan and Peter enriched the royal treasury with another two beautiful crowns – *Diamond Caps (showcase 50)*.

In 1721 Russia was proclaimed an empire. The old coronation ceremony was replaced by a new ritual similar to that used in Western Europe.

One of the first Russian crowns – the *crown of Empress Anna Ivanovna* with diamonds and the unique Chinese red spinel is kept in the Armoury collection.

The Armoury has a priceless collection of *old tsar's thrones* in the *hall 7*.

The most ancient one is the *ivory throne* (16th century) which belonged to Ivan the Terrible. Its wooden frame is covered with ivory plates carved with pictures.

The thrones of tsars Boris Godunov and Mikhail Fyodorovich Romanov

Throne of Tsar Ivan the Terrible.
Western Europe. 16th century.

are decorated with gold plates in a stamped foliage pattern and studded with gem-stones *(showcases 47 and 51)*.

The diamond throne (showcase 47) was presented to Tsar Alexei Mikhailovich by an Armenian trade company for the right of duty-free trade on Rus-

Diamond throne.
Persia. 1659.

sian territory. It is covered with gold and silver plates and encrusted with numerous precious stones, including 800 diamonds.

The young brothers – tsars Ivan and Peter used to sit on a double silver throne *(showcase 48)* specially made for them in 1682 – 1684.

Four-seater carriage.
St.Petersburg. Master K. Bukendal. 1769.

Articles of ceremonial horse decoration displayed in the hall No 8 show the great importance attached to the ritual of tsars' turn-out. Saddles, padded saddles, knee-caps, neck-tassels, lashes, horse-cloths, etc. were made of valuable materials and adorned with gold, silver and semi-precious stones. They were brought from art and crafts centres in Russia and Oriental and West European countries in the 16th – 18th centuries. They are skilfully decorated with coloured enamels, velvet niello and engravings and embossed with high relief. They are real masterpieces of applied art.

Carriages of the 16th – 18th centuries *(hall 9)* is the final section of the exposition. It is one of the best such collections in the world. The carriages on display produced by coach-makers in Russia, Poland, England, France and Austria have both high technical and artistic merits.

The Armoury is one of the richest world treasure-stores. Visitors are amazed not so much by the enormous value of the articles on display, the glitter of gold and the radiance of precious stones, but by the great skill, superb taste and boundless fantasy of the masters who created these wonderful objects.

The Armoury collection belongs not only to Russia, it is a priceless heritage of world culture.

In recent years the Armoury treasures have often been displayed abroad, causing the admiration of connoisseurs in many countries.

Great Imperial crown. 1762.

The Diamond Collection Exhibition was opened on the ground floor of the Armoury in 1967. It is one of the largest collections of jewels in the world. The pride of the Diamond Collection are historical relics, such as state regalia, unique precious stones and articles made thereof. This is a part of the royal treasures which were previously kept in the Diamond Room of the Winter Palace in St.Petersburg.

The exposition shows outstanding works of jewellery art of the 18th – 19th century. There are precious accessories, orders, numerous Russian semiprecious stones, a collection of seven "historic" stones, and rare nuggets of platinum and gold. But the most interesting exhibits are the state imperial regalia.

A real masterpiece is the *Great Imperial crown* made by a talented court

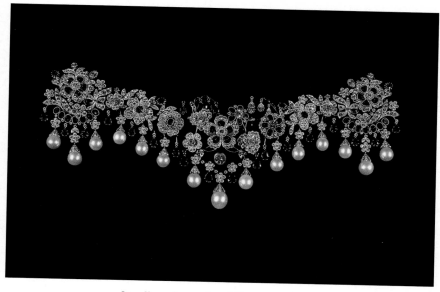

Jewellery decoration "Flower Fantasy".
Masters V. Sitnikov and V. Zhilin. 1991. State Treasury.

jeweller Jeremia Posier for the coronation of Empress Catherine the Great in 1762.

The Great Imperial crown consists of two openwork hemispheres divided by a foliate garland and fastened by a low hoop. The cold sparkling of five thousand diamonds decorating the crown is contrasted by the mat radiance of large beautiful pearls. The crown is also decorated with a rare gem-stone of bright red colour – a precious spinel weighing 398.72 carats. This crown was used at all coronation ceremonies in Russia after Catherine the Great.

A new *orb* was also made in 1762. It is a small gold ball encircled by two bands of large diamonds. Under a diamond cross crowning the orb there is a bright blue Ceylonese sapphire weighing 200 carats.

The gold *sceptre* made in the early 1770s is exquisitely simple. On top of it, under the double-headed eagle, there is the "Orlov" diamond. It is the world's fourth largest diamond (189.62 carats) and the only one with the Indian cut of the 17th century.

The Great Imperial chain of the Order of St.Andrew the First-Called with a cross was placed over the robe worn by the Emperor during the coronation ceremony. The chain consists of 20 open-work links studded with diamonds.

A diamond star for the Great Imperial chain was pinned to the coronation uniform. In its centre there was an inscription laid out in tiny diamonds around the image of a double-headed eagle: "For faith and loyalty" – the motto of the order.

Certain changes were made in the coronation ceremony at the end of the 18th century. In 1797, at the coronation ceremony of Emperor Paul I, the Emperor's wife was also crowned for the first time.

The Diamond Collection has the *Smaller diamond crown* made by the court jewellers, Duval Brothers, in 1801, for the coronation of Yelizaveta Alexeyevna, the wife of Emperor Alexander I. The crown is exquisite and graceful. Traditional in form, it consists of two silver hemispheres with a latticed ornament at the bottom fastened below. Magnificent diamonds decorating the hemispheres seem to emphasize its solemn and strict beauty.

The priceless treasures of the Diamond Collection are a part of the country's national wealth. They are kept under strict control by the state.

THE GREAT KREMLIN PALACE

The term *"Great Kremlin Palace"* applies to a group of buildings, both of civil and religious importance, erected during the 15th-19th centuries. This is a unique architectural complex comprising, besides the Great Kremlin Palace proper, the Facets (or Faceted) Palace, the Tsarina's Golden Palace, the Terem Palace, and a spate of domestic churches. The imperial palace after which the whole ensemble is named features numerous halls where grand receptions were held and a suite of rooms called the "Personal Half".

The earliest structure of the complex is the *Facets Palace*. It was built as the throne hall for the Grand Prince Ivan III, who in 1472 married the Byzantine princess Zoe Sophia Paleologus. Perhaps it was then that the Italian architects Marco Ruffo and Pietro Antonio Solari came to Moscow. At that time, large-scale construction was going on in the Kremlin. It started in 1485 with the building of a new palace for the tsar. The palace was completed in 1508 — after the death of Ivan III, and so his son, Prince Vassily III, was its first owner. In the second half of the 16th and all through the 17th centuries — under Ivan the Terrible, Boris Go-

dunov and the first tsars of the Romanov dynasty — the Facets Palace was rebuilt many times. Only the gala throne hall — the present Facets Palace — has remained of the monumental, sumptuous structure of the 15th century.

The Palace, an imposing rectangular building with a tall ground-floor section, stands facing the Cathedral Square. The eastern facade of the building is done in faceted white limestone, to which the Palace owes its name.

The building changed its appearance several times in the course of the centuries: in 1684, after a fire in the Kremlin, its high pyramidal copper roof was replaced with a lower iron one; the old windows were widened and provided with carved white-stone frames and colonnettes.

Adjoining the Facets Palace is the *Red Porch* with three flights of steps (in old Russian "red" meant "beautiful"). It used to be the main entrance to the throne hall, and it was there that important foreign ambassadors were met with ceremony and conducted inside. Initially, the porch was an open one, but in 1685 Prince Golitsyn had a copper roof installed over it. The lower

The Red Porch
of the Facets Palace.

stair landing was provided with columned archways. In 1842-45 the Red Porch was rebuilt in connection with the construction of the Great Kremlin Palace. Nearly a century later, in 1932, it was completely demolished. All that remained of the original Red Porch was its foundation.

The restoration of the Red Porch began in June 1993, following a decree of the President of the Russian Federation. Taken as a model was the last in a series of restorations carried out by the architect F. Richter in 1842-48 because the necessary documents were preserved in the archives. The restoration work was completed by June 12, 1994, which is Independence Day, a national holiday in Russia.

From the Red Porch a stairway led to the *Holy Vestibule*, an anteroom where visitors used to wait to be received by the tsar.

Very impressive in the Holy Vestibule are lavishly decorated carved white-stone portals and colourful murals on religious and historical themes. The early frescoes had not been preserved: they were repainted by Fyodor Zavyalov in 1847.

The Holy Vestibule.

The *Throne Hall*, the largest at the time, has an area of 500 square metres and a height of nine metres. It has a cross-vaulted ceiling supported by a massive pillar in the middle richly decorated with gilded white-stone ornaments representing dolphins, birds and beasts.

The portal of the Facets Palace is just as richly decorated with stylized floral ornaments and fantastic animals.

The interior of the palace has undergone substantial changes over the last five hundred years. It was first painted at the end of the 16th century during the reign of Tsar Fyodor Ivanovich. By the end of the 17th century the old frescoes were in a poor state, so they were removed and the walls were upholstered in red cloth. In 1881 it was decided to have the Facets Palace painted anew for the coronation of Emperor Alexander III. The painting was done according to the descriptions of 16th-century themes and compositions compiled in 1672 by the well-known painter Simon Ushakov.

In 1882 the Belousov brothers, painters from the village of Palekh, repainted the walls in the traditional style of 16th-century icon-painting. In thirteen circles and semi-circles on the vaults and sloping walls they painted biblical compositions on the creation of the world. On the vaulted ceilings the artists portrayed prophets, forefathers and evangelists with scrolls in their hands. On the walls, in keeping with tradition, they depicted themes from the Bible and Russian history.

Traditionally, the south-east corner was the place where the tsar's throne stood. And so the paintings on the east wall were of special significance. They include themes based on "The Tale of the Princes of Vladimir" which repre-

The Portal of the Facets Palace.
A view from the Holy Vestibule.

sent the historical continuity and consequently the legality of the power of the Moscow princes. This idea was essential to the effort of uniting separate principalities to form a single state. Depicted there are the first princes of the Ryurik dynasty (who were said to have descended from the Roman emperor Augustus), as well as the Kievan Prince Vladimir under whom Rus adopted Christianity in 988 A.D.

The painting on the south wall depicts the presentation of the tsar's regalia to Prince Vladimir Monomachus. Also depicted there are Tsar Fyodor (the son of Ivan the Terrible) and Boris Godunov.

On the sloping walls at the windows there are 24 portraits of Russia's rulers who brought glory to the country. The themes of the frescoes in the Facets Palace prompt one to draw paral-

"Grand Prince Vladimir Svyatoslavovich with His Sons".
A painting on the east wall of the Facets Palace.

lels between the biblical stories and events in Russian history. For instance, the rise to power of the Russian Tsar Boris Godunov and the parable about Joseph the Beautiful from the Old Testament. Depicted on the west wall of the Palace, opposite the tsar's place, are scenes from the didactic parable about the just and unjust judges, painted there as a kind of reminder to the tsar about his responsibilities to his subjects.

The Throne Hall was used for official and ceremonial events. It was there that Meetings of the Land were convened and the Boyars' *Duma* (Council) held its sessions, foreign ambassadors were received and heirs to the throne were named. Also there, in 1552, Tsar Ivan the Terrible celebrated his taking of Kazan, and Peter the Great — his victory over the Swedes at Poltava (1709) and the end of the Northern War (1722). Feasts and receptions were organized with especial luxury: Persian carpets were rolled out; the boyars, dressed in rich brocaded velvet garments, with tall sable hats on their heads, sat on benches placed along the walls; in special cases around the central pillar valuable utensils and vessels were displayed. Foreign visitors were greatly impressed by the sumptuous feasts at the Facets Palace. Describing one of them, the English traveller Richard Chancellor, who was in Moscow as a guest of Tsar Ivan the Terrible, wrote that food was served on gold platters — not only to the tsar but to

A high-level dinner at the Facets Palace.
A lithograph. 1883.

everybody present, while the number of guests at table was around 200. They were served by members of the gentry, all wearing gold-brocaded clothes. One of the ambassadors present there wrote that the tables were densely stood with valuable vessels, and some 140 servants who attended the guests all wore gold-brocaded clothes. Moreover, they changed them three times in the course of the feast.

Today, certain official ceremonies, receptions and other important functions are still held at the Facets Palace.

Situated next to the Facets Palace is the ***Tsarina's Golden Palace***. It was built in the early 16th century for Tsarina Irina Godunova, the wife of Tsar Fyodor Ivanovich (the son of Ivan the Terrible). In the 1580s this palace became the reception premises of the Russian tsarinas. It was given the name "golden" because it was painted in predominantly golden colours. The Gala Hall of the Palace was used by the tsarinas for grand receptions in connection with the marriages and deaths of members of the royal family, as well as for receiving royalty from other countries. The paintings at the Golden Palace show episodes from the lives of the Kievan Princess Olga (the first Russian Christian princess), St. Dinara, the Georgian tsarina who defeated the Persian tsar in the 11th century, and the righteous Feodora, the wife of the Byzantine emperor Theophilius.

At the beginning of the 17th century, after the fires and destruction of the "troubled period", the Golden Palace, like all other palaces of the Kremlin, was in poor condition. During the following decades the wall paintings of the Golden Palace were repeatedly renovated. For instance, in 1796 its walls were repainted in oils to celebrate the coronation of Emperor Paul I.

The Kremlin restorers have done complex and painstaking work to uncover the original paintings of the Golden Palace and to restore them to their initial splendour.

The **Terem Palace** was built by order of Tsar Mikhail Fyodorovich Romanov in the inner courtyard of the Great Kremlin Palace in 1635-36 by the Russian architects Bazhen Ogurtsov, Antipy Sharutin and Larion Ushakov on the site of the earlier palaces built for Vassily III and Ivan the Terrible.

The Terem Palace is a real gem of early Russian architecture. The fabulous building has five storeys. Its basement was used for household cellars and storerooms.

On the first floor there were workshops where royal garments were made and kept. The tsar's and tsarina's living quarters were on the second and third floors. The top floor presents the so-called *Upper Terem* which has a gilded roof and stands on the flat roof of the Terem Palace proper. It has a gallery called *gulbishche* (a gallery built on the basement level around a house) round it, and it was built for the sons of Tsar Mikhail Fyodorovich Romanov.

The decor of the palace is representative of typically Russian tracery-like architecture: its carved and painted ornaments are reminiscent of embroidery. The carved decorative elements on the brick walls of the palace are made of white stone. The builders used all the materials, forms and decorative elements at their disposal. The portals, cornices and window-frames are all covered with white-stone carvings, painted ornaments and colourful relief tiles. The double windows of the upper floors, with their triple arcades and hanging decorative tie-pieces, are crowned by triangular frontons propped by pilasters. Their broad surfaces are filled in with interlaced floral patterns and figures of double-headed eagles and other mythological birds and beasts. The palace was rebuilt many times over the past centuries. The original paintings were restored during the 1960s.

The Upper Stone Courtyard of the Terem Palace, prior to its rebuilding in the 19th century, was an open place surrounded by a parapet with the *Golden Railing*. This fine piece of craftsmanship, gilded and painted, with its delicately interlaced spirals and fairy-tale beasts is indicative of the author's rich imagination. In the past, one could see in the passages of the Terem Palace

The Terem Palace.

many such railings forged of iron or cast of copper.

A carved white-stone staircase leads to the gala halls of the Terem Palace. In the olden days it was called the *Golden Porch*. The staircase has two landings — an upper and a lower one. An arch above the upper landing is adorned with a decorative tie-piece in the shape of a lion's head. The steps and the banisters are decorated with intricate carvings, and the walls — with colourful paintings. Stone lions sitting on their haunches "guard" the entrance to the palace.

The tsar's living quarters on the third floor consist of a suite of five adjoining rooms. Very few guests were given the honour of being admitted to "the tsar's presence in the upper rooms". The first of the rooms was called the *Front Vestibule* or *Refectory*. In the

*The Upper Landing
of the Terem Palace.*

morning the boyars gathered there to wait for the tsar, and sometimes banquets were held there.

In the second room — the *Council* or *Duma Chamber* — the tsar met with the boyars.

The third room, the most majestic of all, called the *Throne Hall*, was the tsar's study. The purple walls of the Hall are adorned with the gilded emblems of all the Russian territories.

The next room is the *Bedroom*. It gives access to the *Prayer Room*, covered with the painted figures of saints. Here are 17th-18th century icons in two gilded carved encasements (*kiots*).

As was the custom, the tsar got up very early — about 4 a.m., and at once he proceeded to the Prayer Room (or the Cross Chamber). After saying his prayers and getting properly dressed,

he sent one the boyars to the tsarina's quarters *"to enquire about her health and whether she had slept well"*. Sometimes, he went himself to greet the tsarina, and together they proceeded to one of the Kremlin churches to attend the morning service there. After church the tsar went to the Front Vestibule. There he met with the waiting boyars, and together they discussed affairs of state.

The boyars were obliged to show up at the palace every morning. This was done in accordance with very strict rules: one could not come, for instance, bearing arms, or feeling unwell, or being in a foul mood and using "improper language".

The first half of the day was usually devoted to a session with the boyars, consideration of applications and requests, and the giving of audiences to foreign ambassadors.

On weekdays, after the midday meal, the tsar slept for three hours and then went to the bath-house — this was a must. Afterwards, he might attend an entertainment, such as a bear show or a fist fight. Along towards evening the boyars again congregated at the palace. Sometimes, following a prayer service, affairs of state were considered, and sometimes a Duma session was held. But more often than not, that period of time was devoted to amusement.

All the rooms in the Terem Palace are rather small and low-ceilinged and about the same size; each has three windows and a vaulted ceiling. The supports of the vaults are decorated with bas-reliefs depicting birds, beasts and double-headed eagles. The doorways are rather low and decorated with painted and gilded stone carving. In those days the floor was laid in oak blocks and then covered first with felt and then with green or red cloth. On ceremonial occasions carpets were spread on top of the cloth. The stained glass effect in the windows was achieved with the help of squares and triangles of coloured foil, and the wooden window-sills were intricately carved.

Tiled stoves are an essential element of the interior of the rooms. The tiles are of various shapes and sizes, glazed, multicoloured and artistically decorated. The ornamental patterns and motifs of the tiles combine to present a colourful composition. Usually, there is a flower or a rosette in the middle, and the border is filled in with scrolls and twining plants. The existing stoves were restored in the mid-19th century

in accordance with old models; so the patterns reproduced are very close to the original, but the colours are considerably distorted.

The furniture in early Russian living rooms was rather scant and simple. The benches along the walls were used both for sitting and sleeping on, and they often had built-in chests underneath. A few chairs and cupboards were also present at times.

By the early 17th century, however, there were beds with beautiful baldachins in the tsar's rooms, carved gilded armchairs and Western-style wardrobes.

The original paintings on the walls of the tsar's rooms have not survived. One can form an idea of what they were like from descriptions left by contemporaries. Here is one of them: *"The wall paintings were distinct for their bright colours, an abundance of gilt and intricate ornamentation."*

The tsar's rooms were repainted nearly every year. The wall paintings one can see today are what was restored in the mid-19th century on the basis of some sketches made by Fyodor Solntsev, a member of the Academy of Art. The tsar's rooms were decorated with even greater luxury during receptions of foreign ambassadors. This was done to impress foreigners and convince them of the might of the Russian state and its sovereign. On such occasions Persian carpets and colourful fabrics were rolled out for the guest to walk on. Numerous guards and servants dressed in sumptuous clothes, issued them by the treasury for the occasion, lined the passages and stairways of the palace.

Despite the numerous alterations and additions, the Terem Palace has large-

The Tsar's Study of the Terem Palace.
Painted by F. Dreger from Shadursky's drawing. 1851.

ly preserved its initial appearance.

As mentioned at the beginning, the Great Kremlin Palace complex includes a group of small **domestic churches** built in the period from the 14th to the 17th centuries.

Originally, there were eleven of them, but only six have remained after the numerous reconstructions of the 18th and 19th centuries. They are: the Saviour's Upper Cathedral, the Church of the Crucifixion, the Church of the Resurrection of Christ, the Church of Saint Catherine, the Church of the Nativity of the Virgin, and the Church of the Resurrection of Lazarus.

The oldest of them is *the Church of the Nativity of the Virgin*. Built in 1393 on the order of Princess Yevdokia, the widow of Prince Dmitry Donskoi, it was renamed *the Church of the Resurrection of Lazarus* in the early 16th century. In 1514, the Italian architect Alevisio Novy built a new church over the old one which was named the Nativity Church. Subsequently, the upper church was rebuilt many times. But the greatest alterations were caused by the construction of the Great Kremlin Palace in the 19th century. It was then that the walls of the Church were repainted in oils.

The Saviour's Upper Cathedral was built in 1635-36 as the domestic church of Tsar Mikhail Fyodorovich. One of the main attractions of this church is

The cupolas of the domestic churches.

its gilded carved-wood iconostasis created by Russian painters in the second half of the 17th century. The most remarkable of the icons are those painted by Fyodor Zubov in his characteristically free and festive manner.

Also quite remarkable is the interior of *the Church of the Resurrection of Christ* (1680-81). Its iconostasis with its traceried carvings in high relief and glittering gilt elements is strikingly beautiful and has a rather unusual colour scheme. Carved details covered with coloured lacquer are laid over a green-blue surface. Such a combination of painting and carving in high relief cannot be found anywhere else, and it has no parallel among any of the surviving 17th-century works.

In 1681, by the order of Tsar Fyodor Alexeyevich, a small Church of the Crucifixion was erected next to the Saviour's Upper Cathedral. Its magnif-

icent iconostasis was made by the talented icon-painter Vassily Poznansky and is quite unique. It contains icons made in a rare appliqué technique: the faces of the saints are painted in oils and the rest — clothes, attributes and the background are made out of fabric.

One of the six domestic churches of the Great Kremlin Palace is devoted to St. Catherine. It was built by the architect John Taler in 1627-28 for the tsarinas and the princesses. The 1737 fire destroyed its interior, but in the 19th century it was restored.

In 1683, four domestic churches were united by a common roof crowned by eleven cupolas with magnificent openwork gold crosses. The round bases on which the cupolas rest are decorated with colourful tiles. The gilded roof with eleven domes presents a striking view from the Cathedral Square.

The Great Kremlin Palace.
A painting by S. Shukhvostov. 1849.

The ***Great Kremlin Palace*** proper is a masterpiece of Russian architecture. It was built on Borovitsky Hill in the south-west part of the Kremlin grounds, on the site of the earlier residence of grand princes and later of the tsars.

In the Middle Ages in Russia the term "palace" (earlier *"terem"*) meant a complex of buildings with living quarters, halls for receptions, court churches, workshops, and auxiliary premises. The terems of princes were first mentioned in the mid-14th century and associated with Prince Ivan Kalita. The inexorable time and numerous fires did not spare the Kremlin's old buildings. By the end of the 18th century many of

them had fallen into decay. The construction of a new palace which would meet the requirements of the royal court began in 1838 and continued for eleven years.

The Great Kremlin Palace faces the Moskva River. A group of architects, headed by the famous St. Petersburg architect K.A. Thon (1794-1881), who was known for his ability to build quickly and well, was given the task of designing and constructing the building. Such outstanding Moscow architects as F.F. Richter, N.I. Chichagov and P.A. Gerasimov also took part in the project. They managed to cope with the complicated task of uniting several buildings belonging to different styles and different periods (14th-17th centuries) in a single complex. As was mentioned earlier, this complex comprised, besides the new 19th-century building, the Facets Palace, the Terem Palace, the Tsarina's Golden Palace, and the domestic churches. Although its interior design and plan are quite modern, its exterior is done in a style reminiscent of the centuries past. The traditional approach is clearly seen in the application of decorative techniques. The palace has carved white-stone pediments and double-arched platbands on the window-openings with hanging tie-pieces in the centre (as in the 17th-century terems). The main and the eastern faces of the building have terraces in the style of an early Russian *gulbishche* (a gallery built on the basement level around a house). The main entrance and the arched recesses of the south side of the building match well. The palace has a figured roof with a cupola on top.

For its size, magnificence and grandeur the Great Kremlin Palace was the equal of many other 19th-century palaces in Western Europe. Its main facade is 125 metres long and 44 metres high. There are about 700 rooms with a total area of 20,000 square metres. There are three tiers of windows but only two storeys: the gala halls on the second floor have two tiers of windows. The socle of the brick walls is faced with grey stone, while the cornices and platbands — with white limestone.

The Great Kremlin Palace is a typical example of late 19th-century Russian architecture. The interior of the palace, which incorporates elements of various styles — from baroque to classicism, is still in very good condition. Involved in decorating the interior were eminent artists and sculptors — F.G. Solntsev, I.P. Vitali, P.K. Klodt and O.V. Loganovsky. Russia's best factories and workshops were engaged in making the furniture and elements of decor for the palace. Such elements were real works of art made from malachite, jasper, marble, granite and rare varieties of wood.

A great number of porcelain and bronze articles, clocks, crystal chandeliers, artistically made doors and parquetry comprise an ensemble reflecting the tastes and esthetic standards of 19th-century high society in Russia.

The second floor of the Great Kremlin Palace is occupied by gala reception halls named Georgievsky, Vladimirsky, Andreyevsky, Yekaterininsky and Alexandrovsky. These names correspond to the tsarist Russian orders, whose elements are included in the stucco mouldings in each hall. The upholstery is coloured in accordance with the ribbon of the respective order.

The *Georgievsky* (St. George's) *Hall* is the largest and best-known of the gala halls. It was conceived as a hall of glory of the Russian army and is devoted to the Order of St. George, one of the highest military decorations instituted by Empress Catherine the Great in 1769. The atmosphere of the hall is majestic and solemn. The light from the two tiers of windows floods the room. Visitors are struck by its enormous size: the room is 61 metres long, 20.5 metres wide, and 17.5 metres high. Relief work, sculpture and gilded bronze decorations adorn the white walls and the vaulted ceiling. The hall glitters in the light of the tiered open-work chandeliers and wall lamps set all along the cornices. The huge

The Georgievsky Hall.

vaulted ceiling of the hall is supported by 18 massive pillars with twisted columns cast in zinc attached to them. Above their capitals one can see sculptured figures — the allegoric images of the regions which joined the Rus-sian state between the late 15th and early 19th centuries (the work of the sculptor I.P. Vitali). The names of the regiments awarded the Order of St. George and the names of the Knights of St. George are inscribed in gold letters on the marble plates on the walls and pillars. Among them are the names of the heroes of the Patriotic War of 1812: A.V. Suvorov, M.I. Kutuzov, P.I. Bagration, V.V. Ushakov and P.S. Nakhimov.

The furniture, carved and gilded, is upholstered in watered silk of the same colour as the decoration ribbon. There are relief images of the symbols of the Order of St. George (the cross and the star) in the carved ornamentation on the walls and the ceiling. In the semicirculars of the transversal walls there are high reliefs depicting St. George on horseback (the work of the sculptor P.K. Klodt).

The magnificent parquetry, designed by F.G. Solntsev, is made up of 20 valuable types of wood and looks like an enormous carpet. Today, the Georgievsky Hall is the site of celebration meetings, award ceremonies and diplomatic receptions.

Two gala halls, Alexandrovsky and Andreyevsky, follow the Georgievsky Hall on the south side of the Great Kremlin Palace.

The *Andreyevsky* (St. Andrew's) *Hall* was devoted to the Order of St. Andrew instituted by Peter the Great in 1698. It was the Russian emperors' Throne Hall. Their throne stood at the east wall. On ceremonial occasions higher military officials met there. The walls of the hall were upholstered in blue watered silk (the colour of the Order of St. Andrew's ribbon) and decorated with the Order's insignia. Over the door there were the emperors' monograms: those of Peter the Great, the founder of the Order; Paul I, who instituted the status of the Order; and Nicholas I, who built the Andreyevsky Hall. Over the windows there were the emblems of Russia's gubernias and regions. The parquet floor was made by Miller according to F. Solntsev's design. The interior was decorated with two mantel-pieces made of violet-grey jasper. There were no chairs in the hall since no one was supposed to sit in the emperor's presence.

The *Alexandrovsky* (St. Alexander's) *Hall* was named so in honour of the Order of St. Alexander Nevsky instituted by Catherine I in 1725.

The walls of the hall were faced with rose-coloured imitation marble, and its spherical cupola was decorated with the Order's symbols and state emblems.

Between the gilt twisted columns there were the emblems of Russia's gubernias and regions. Paintings by Moller, presenting episodes from the life of St. Alexander Nevsky, hung on the walls. There were glass-panel doors and windows in the back wall. The hall was decorated with four marble mantelpieces and gilded chairs upholstered in velvet the colour of the Order's ribbon. The upholstery on the back of the chairs bore the star of the Order.

In 1934 both the Andreyevsky and Alexandrovsky Halls were completely altered: they were merged to form a single hall in which the USSR Supreme Soviet sessions and Communist Party congresses were held. The magnificent decor of the old halls had been destroyed.

At present, both the Andreyevsky and the Alexandrovsky Halls are being restored to their original appearance.

Next to the Georgievsky Hall is the *Vladimirsky* (St. Vladimir's) *Hall*, devoted to the Order of St. Vladimir and instituted by Catherine the Great in 1782. It was built on the site of the open

The Andreyevsky Hall.
A painting by K.A. Ukhtomsky. 1849.

Boyar Gallery of the 17th century, and it serves as a link between the palace buildings of the 15th-17th centuries and the later, 19th-century ones. It is an octagonal room with cut corners and big broad arches in the lower part. Above them is a tier of smaller arches where the choir gallery is located. The walls and pilasters are faced with rose-coloured imitation marble. The cupola-shaped vault is decorated with gilt ornaments and symbols of the Order of

The Alexandrovsky Hall.
A painting by K.A. Ukhtomsky. 1849.

St. Vladimir (a red-enamelled gold cross and a star).

During the day the Hall is lit by the sun shining through the vaulted cupola, and in the evening a large bronze chandelier lights it up.

The pattern of the parquet floor, which is made of rare varieties of wood, is simply superb (the work of F. Solntsev). The watered silk upholstery of the furniture corresponds to the colours of the Order of St. Vladimir's ribbon.

The Vladimirsky Hall.
A painting by K.A. Ukhtomsky. 1849.

On the second floor level of the west wing of the Great Kremlin Palace there is *the Gala Half* suite, comprising the Yekaterininsky Hall, the Gala Reception Hall, the Bedroom and the Walnut Cloakroom.

The *Yekaterininsky* (St. Catherine's) *Hall* used to be the Russian empresses' throne room. It was so named in honour of the Order of St. Catherine instituted by Emperor Peter the Great in 1714.

The Yekaterininsky Hall.
A painting by K.A. Ukhtomsky. 1849.

The cross-vaulted ceiling of the hall is supported by two massive pylons. The pilasters are decorated with bronze capitals and malachite mosaics. The walls are covered with grey watered silk with a red edge (the colour of the decoration ribbon). There are the symbols of the order against a red background and the motto "For the Love of Fatherland".

The gilded stucco moulding on the vaults and the cornices, the gilt carved doors with the Order's symbols, the gilt bronze chandeliers and the crystal candelabra on pedestals of red French marble — all combine to create a festive atmosphere. And the parquet floor is a real work of art.

Next to Yekaterininsky is the **Gala Reception Hall**. The vaulted ceiling of this semi-circular room is painted with floral ornament (the work of the artist D. Artary).

Both the walls and the furniture are upholstered in golden-green brocade. The tables and the doors are made in the Boulle style (the famous French wood-carver Boulle worked at the

The Gala Reception Hall.
A painting by K.A. Ukhtomsky. 1850.

court of Louis XIV). The furniture is encrusted with copper, tin, tortoise-shell and valuable types of wood.

The niches in the walls are revetted with white imitation marble. In the niches are porcelain torchères finely painted in the Chinese style.

Quite remarkable are an enormous candelabrum which holds 60 candles and flower vases made in the Japanese style.

Both real and imitation marble of different colours — white, rosy-grey and green — was widely used in the interior decoration of the *Main Bedroom*. The most outstanding features of the room are its greenish-grey marble columns and bluish-green mantel-piece.

These are fine examples of Russian stone-carving done at Yekaterinburg in the Urals.

The clock and the candelabra on the mantel-shelf were made by French craftsmen in the 19th century. The walls and the gilded furniture were upholstered in bright crimson damask. The damask, velvet and brocade used for the walls, the furniture and the curtains were manufactured at G.G. Sapozhnikov's textile mill in Moscow. The fabrics produced by this factory were internationally known and considered the best in Russia.

The last in the suite of rooms of the Gala Half is the *Walnut Cloakroom*. Its walls and ceiling are faced with

The Main Bedroom.
A painting by K.A. Ukhtomsky. 1851.

walnut. No glue or paste was used in the panelling of the room. This work was done by the Moscow craftsman I. Hertz. The room is lit by an alabaster chandelier with a fine herbal pattern cut on its thin milk-white facets. The chandelier was made in Santino Campioni's workshop in 1845-48. Its shape was inspired by antique models imitating which was a very popular trend in the 19th century.

The royal family's living apartments were called *Personal Half* and are on the ground floor. Massive pillars divide the rooms into cosy compartments. They are made even more comfortable by the skilful arrangement of richly inlaid furniture. Gilded stucco mouldings

in each of the rooms add to the festive atmosphere. Damask in motley colours was used for the curtains; the upholstery of the furniture and walls was coordinated in colour with the mantelpieces, creating an atmosphere of inimitable beauty.

Each of the seven large rooms — the Dining Room, the Drawing Room, the Empress's Study, the Emperor's Study, the Waiting Room, the Bedroom and the Boudoir — and four small connecting rooms are a unique example of the 19th-century interior. The specific atmosphere of each room is attained by a skilful selection of porcelain, crystal and bronze, and unique and varied furniture and upholstery.

The Personal Half suite of rooms begins with the **Dining Room**, the largest and brightest of them all. It is adorned in the Renaissance style, its walls and ceiling are covered with imitation white marble. Coloured panels hang on the walls and there are many marble sculptures, porcelain vases and torchères imitating ancient Roman models. Marble vases on top of high pedestals are in the niches, and these vases are decorated with scenes from Greek and Roman mythology. There are two porcelain vases which are truly outstanding for their beauty and classical proportions. Painted on them are some episodes from Russian history.

All the rooms, starting with the Dining Room, are divided into two parts, differing in size and designation. The front part with the windows and the fireplace was the larger and more official, while the back part was the smaller and intended for rest and recreation.

The rococo style is quite evident in the interior decoration of the **Empress's Drawing Room**: the light colours, the elegance of the stucco moulding and floral patterns and the curved forms of the furniture are the distinctive features of the room. Porcelain articles are everywhere, including flower vases and candelabra. There is also a large central chandelier in the form of a bouquet laid with pineapples, a symbol of prosperity. Russian craftsmen from the Imperial Porcelain Works in St. Petersburg were famed for their skill in modelling porcelain flowers.

White and coloured marble and gilt were widely used in decorating the **Empress's Study**. There is crimson damask on the walls, and the furniture is inlaid with tortoise-shell, gilt copper and brass in the Boulle style.

The centrepiece of the **Boudoir** is a magnificent fireplace faced with small pieces of green Urals malachite carefully chosen in colour and pattern to create the impression of a monolith. The craftsmen working at the Demidov and Turchaninov factories in the Urals in the 19th century attained perfection in finishing malachite. Gilt medallions adorn the fireplace. They depict sirens, cartouches, rosettes and herbal patterns.

Next to the Boudoir are the *Emperor's Bedroom* and *Study*. These rooms are decorated in stricter style which is more in keeping with their function.

The walls and the simple furniture of the **Bedroom** are upholstered in blue damask. Three colours — blue, white and gold — are prevalent in the interior decoration.

The ceiling is painted with bouquets and thin foliate volutes. There is a white-marble fireplace with a traditional clock and a candelabrum on its mantel-piece.

The **Emperor's Study** has a strictly formal appearance. Its walls are panelled in light-coloured ash; the furniture is upholstered in green leather. Above the fireplace, in the space between the windows, there is a mirror. Stucco mouldings and a chandelier in art nouveau style adorn the ceiling.

The furniture in the **Waiting Room** is upholstered in "velvet on satin". The velvet pile is clipped in a peculiar manner to create a play of light and shadow: the velvet changes its shades depending on the lighting. This and other fabrics were manufactured at G.G. Sapozhnikov's factory in Moscow.

The Great Kremlin Palace is a unique historical and cultural monument. It reveals fully the artistic manner and national peculiarities of Russian craftsmen of various epochs.

Today, the Great Kremlin Palace, the residence of the President of the Russian Federation is the centre of the country's political life. It is there that summit meeting, diplomatic receptions, the signing of international agreements and award presentation ceremonies are held.

And so, our brief survey of the Moscow Kremlin has come to a close. We have told you about its history, the architectural monuments and works of art being carefully preserved there, and the priceless relics which are the national asset of Russia.

We hope that your visit to the Moscow Kremlin will help you to learn much more about our country, its history and culture.

Glossary

Arkatura — a non-functional closed or false arcade serving as an ornament; a decorative band of blind arches.

Barmy — part of the regalia of the Moscow tsars; a broad collar made of black silk overlaid with gold and jewels.

Boyar — member of the highest social and political class in Russia until Peter the Great established the "Table of Ranks" (1722), which made rank technically dependent on service position.

Chin — order, rank, different orders of angels or saints.

Dyak — secretary (word of the same origin as the English "deacon").

Kalita — money bag.

Khory — gallery, galleries.

Kiot — a niche, a frame or cupboard in which one or more icons may be housed.

Klobuk — cloth covering a priest's head-dress.

Kokoshnik — originally a structural feature, a series of round or pointed arches arranged in receding tiers for the purpose of supporting the elements of the superstructure. Later it developed into a purely decorative feature.

Kukol — a monk's head-dress.

Mitra — mitre, head-dress of a bishop.

Panagia — a medallion bearing a sacred picture that is worn on the breast of a bishop of the Eastern Orthodox Church.

Panikadilo — chandelier, lustre in the form of an open-work disk.

Papert — covered or uncovered gallery circling the church on three sides.

Plashchanitsa — an embroidered representation of the dead Christ carried in procession on Good Friday.

Pridel — chapel (lateral).

Prikaz — an administrative body developed for the permanent discharge of the duties or functions a boyar was ordered to discharge, a bureau; juridical office of the Muscovite state in charge of special government activities or of governing certain regions. These bodies were replaced by the Collegia of Peter the Great.

Raka — in the Christian church a large box for keeping the remains of saints.

Riza — priest's drapery worn during mass.

Sakkos — a vestment resembling a dalmatic worn by a bishop in the Eastern Orthodox Church during the liturgy.

Sion — a vessel for eucharistic wafers, usually in the form of a church or shrine with cupolas surmounted by a cross.

Skit — a small monastery with regulations stricter than those in an ordinary monastery.

Skladen — a folding icon.

Zakomara — the parapet over the extrados of the vaulting, conforming in outline to the type and number of vaults, and thus dividing the parapet into several arched sections.

Contents

FOR NOTES

FOR NOTES

FOR NOTES

МОСКОВСКИЙ КРЕМЛЬ
Путеводитель.
На английском языке.

Авторы текста
Н. Владимирская, Р. Костикова, И. Родимцева.
Перевод на английский
А. Крыжанский, Е. Хазанов, Л. Ходырев.
Иллюстрации и фото
Фототека Государственного историко-культурного
музея-заповедника «МОСКОВСКИЙ КРЕМЛЬ»;
А. Усанов.
Подбор иллюстраций
А. Дементьева

Изд. лиц. № 020842 от 09.12.93. Подписано в печать 20.08.99.
Формат 70х100/16. Печать офсетная. Печ. л. 8,25. Уч.-изд. л. 10,6.
Бумага Galerie Art. Гарнитура Times New Roman.
Тираж 20.000 экз. Цена договорная.

Государственный историко-культурный
музей-заповедник «МОСКОВСКИЙ КРЕМЛЬ»
103073 Москва, Кремль

The Moscow Kremlin
State Historical and Cultural Museum-Monument.
103073 Moscow, Russia

Made in Finland by OY ScanWeb AB in cooperation with Sofinta Co.Ltd.